₵LASHES

Adventures in Dating through Menopause

MICHELLE CHURCHILL

For more information contact:
Riverdale Avenue Books
5676 Riverdale Avenue
Riverdale, NY 10471

www.riverdaleavebooks.com
Interior layout: www.formatting4U.com
Cover by Scott Carpenter

ISBN: 978-1-62601-006-2

Originally published as *I Thought I Grew Up* by Michelle Churchill © 2009 iUniverse

First Edition December 2012

Coming of Age Again

I am middle-aged.

I am an older woman.

People call me "ma'am."

I call underwear foundation, and, after years of the weight of gravity on my body, I now look better with foundation than without it.

I am a much different woman than I was when I moved to New York more than twenty-five years ago. I was a fresh-faced Midwestern girl with little life experience. The wildest thing I had ever done was drink sloe gin in the college dorm room of a young man who wore pink leopard print spandex pants like Rod Stewart. I let him kiss the sloe gin from my lips and then went running back to the safety of my own dorm room.

As soon as I could, I fled my North Dakota home and ran to New York. Seeking fame and fortune as a serious actress, I imagined I would quickly be discovered and, just as quickly, my career would skyrocket. I would become a household name.

Things didn't proceed quite as I had imagined,

but landing in a city where I didn't know a living soul and where no one knew me was enough to set me free. I managed to get myself on the A-list at New York's hot spots. I dyed my auburn locks amazing shades of platinum with soft pink and gold rinses. I sang in clubs that ranged from CBGB to the Playboy Club. New York City and I embraced each other.

I was where I belonged. I came of age for the first time in New York, and now I find myself coming of age again.

Menopause

I am in menopause.

I am at my beginning.

Again, I have come of age.

We all do it. We all do it differently: hormone replacement therapy, hot flashes, loss of sex drive, increased sex drive, the tragedy of new facial hair, fear of bone loss, and antidepressants. None of us knows what will come next and very few of us share our secrets. I have spent the last few years discussing these issues with girlfriends. While we have shocked and surprised each other, we have also found comfort in our common stories.

After years of being single and keeping my eyes on nothing but my career, it was time to take control of my body and myself. I had just gone through a record emotional dry spell. I felt very alone, but I imagined I wasn't in a place so different from other women. We women in the workplace spend years losing ourselves in order to gain career advancement that, even if it does come, is never as satisfying as we thought. We arrive at a time in our late thirties and through our forties when men take second place to career and either don't notice us or assume we must be a lesbian because we haven't noticed them. It is the time when a woman gains a reputation in the workplace for being a bitch.

Don't get me wrong. We can be bitches during this time, but for the most part we are really more misunderstood than bitchy. Despite the fact that our bodies and minds are going through a change no man can ever comprehend, we remain relatively level-headed and make incredibly sound decisions. We simply will not do it with the same compassionate and loving smile we had in our twenties. We can no longer tolerate the expectation that we will relinquish to a man the credit for a job well done.

Every woman should know that the dry spell is over when you release yourself and allow yourself to say the "m" word. With or without the big job, a loving partner in your life, or personal wealth, it happens – menopause.

How It Began

I had an excellent job in the legal and technology industry. I was one of the top people in my field, earning well over six figures, and I continued to receive raises and promotions. At the same time, I was sixty pounds overweight.

I was fat.

I'd secretly slip off to stores for plus-sized women and promptly cut out the tags when I got home so no one – not even me – would know what size they were or where they had been purchased. I no longer owned a single piece of clothing that didn't have some sort of elastic in it. I suffered from stress-triggered insomnia. I had not dated in at least ten years and I had even stopped having sex with myself.

With little or no warning, I hit the glass ceiling. It was clear to everyone but me that I could go no further in my career without a penis of my very own. I confess I had considered buying one and just putting it on the table in front of me when attending meetings in conference rooms or possibly displaying my purchased penis prominently in my office, but good judgment got the better of me.

A younger man was hired to be my boss. I frantically tried to keep myself afloat while educating him about the nature of my job. The next thing I knew, my phone rang and human resources called for an immediate meeting. They suggested that I seemed "unhappy" and should perhaps go. I remember nothing else but getting up and walking out the door feeling numb. In that moment, I suddenly found myself unemployed and was nearly as stunned as everyone around me was.

Brought on by a combination of stress release and hormones run amok, I had a period that lasted two months. It wasn't just a little spotting here and there. Little demons had crawled inside my body and turned on a spigot. I should have gone to the doctor, but since I was sure I was dying, what difference would that make? I mentioned it in passing to a couple of girlfriends, but I didn't tell them the true extent of what was happening with my body and of my terror. In fact, I didn't confess the extent of that episode to anyone for nearly two years.

So there I was, unemployed, single, and staring menopause in the face. I had absolutely no idea what I was supposed to do, so I did nothing for six months. Even if you can't afford to take real time off when you lose a job, you will still experience time off because you will have a blackout phase of about six months. You'll have no recollection of what you did, how you got anywhere, or what decisions you made. Make no true-life decisions when your life path changes course dramatically. Not to worry, at the end of the new path you will find your mind; I believe I found mine.

In a moment of clarity, I decided that the thing to

do was to change again. I decided my new path to glory would be selling real estate. I changed careers, and my hours became as irregular as my period. At the same time, I quit drinking coffee and smoking cigarettes.

Despite all the turmoil in my life, I had never looked better. People stopped me on the street to tell me how great I looked! Strangers wondered if I'd share the name of my surgeon. I was stunned. My big secret was sleep. I was sleeping for the first time in fifteen years. I lost sixty pounds without dieting. I looked as if I'd had surgery, but I am here to tell you there were no bills and no pain, only blissful sleep.

It was time to write a whole new chapter in my life. Emerging hot flashes notwithstanding, I felt ready.

Ready, Willing, and Much More Stable

For months I have been, for want of a better word, distracted. As my menstrual cycle became more irregular, I have physically and emotionally gone back in time to puberty – when my cycle was first irregular. Certainly my hormones were as wacky now as they were then, perhaps for a different reason, but the result was the same. I could think of nothing but men. I wouldn't say sex, even though that was true most of the time, but I thought about their legs and the hair on their bodies. I thought of how their hands would feel holding mine. It was never really personal, just an ever-present desire to have male contact in any way I could.

So how does a single woman of forty-eight living in New York City accomplish that male closeness? Raging hormones were skewing my judgment. Going out to bars would be disastrous. Bookstores? Grocery stores? Work? No. This is New York City and most of the men I have met over the years are either gay, married, or both.

I decided to turn to the only thing I had a true relationship with over the last ten years, my computer.

I signed up for every online dating service I could find that didn't seem pornographic in nature. They all work differently. Some are black holes of mystery where information goes in and never comes back out. Some take the information and decide who you should possibly meet. This particular system seems even less reliable than my friends' feeble attempts to set me up over the years. Then there are those dating services where you can perform searches, send flirtatious notes, or, if you're feeling truly bold, an email.

What I found interesting about meeting men on the Internet is that it didn't seem to work that differently than in real life. The men do the approaching while I search and review profiles, and occasionally send a brief message to potential dates. Perhaps it was an initial shyness or maybe just being out of practice, but I felt it was my duty to wait.

The emails began. At first, I was surprised. There were young men and old men alike showing interest. What were they looking for? A date? Marriage? Sex? Have they read my profile? The picture actually looks like me. Are they blind? Did they actually read my age?

My First Date

Within forty-eight hours, the first viable flirtation came in. Mr. Handsome was about my age and attractive with a similar career path. Since, unlike me, he had a penis of his own, Mr. Handsome was still gainfully employed. I was optimistic. After the exchange of several email pleasantries, we agreed to meet for a date. I was nervous because it had been so long since I had been on an actual dinner date – I can't even recall having had a date in the last decade – I wasn't sure how to act or what to wear. I was a forty-eight-year-old woman who had to have a girlfriend come over to help me pick out what to wear. A couple hours passed while I modeled possible outfits and worked on hair and makeup.

I was beside myself. My girlfriend suggested a drink, but I decided it would be wrong to be drunk at the beginning of my date. I considered taking a Valium, but realized that could end badly as the evening progressed.

I decided that a smart cocktail upon arrival at the restaurant would ease my nerves enough. If it was really bad, I'd just skip dinner and come home. My makeup was perfect, and my hair looked good. I waited for Mr. Handsome to pick me up for dinner.

So now comes my first lesson learned. Men do not always represent themselves in an honest fashion, especially when it's done anonymously. While I did somewhat recognize him when he arrived, the picture must have been old. Very old. An entirely different person came to pick me up. He was older, grayer, and heavier. Amazingly, he seemed completely unaware of it. He chatted easily about the wonders of himself and, although I still can't figure out how he worked it into the conversation, Mr. Handsome even referred to his small ass. His ass, by the way, was roughly the size of Iowa. As if that weren't enough, he was rude to the wait staff. It was the longest dinner on record. I think the feeling was mutual. I never heard from him again.

The Mrs. Robinson Fantasy

The emails came pouring in. Thank God, most online dating services allow you to initially communicate anonymously and block unwanted attempts at communication. I had a couple of flirtations that seemed as if they might go somewhere, but it was still too soon to tell.

Then along came an entirely different kind of flirtation. He was cute, fair, and younger than springtime. He began with what seemed like a sincere question about my online profile. He wondered if I truly loved dinosaur bones. We exchanged several anonymous emails revealing only the information we had chosen to share and what was supposed to be a recent photo. He was only thirty-six. I wondered why he liked me, and I asked him why he had chosen to flirt with a woman so much older. Was he typically attracted to older women?

He said I was beautiful and the instant messaging conversations began.

The first instant message was more than flirtatious, but it didn't cross the line. He was funny, charming, and sexy. The following night, we had another instant messaging encounter. This time, the tone was a bit beyond flirtation and I enjoyed his boldness. I agreed to meet him for a drink and gave him my phone number.

Regression

The funny thing about getting older is that we suddenly find ourselves doing the things we did when we were younger, like slumber parties. In celebration of my forty-eighth birthday, I had plans for an overnight getaway with a fellow menopausal woman. We ran off to a bed-and-breakfast. Her fantastic husband stayed behind to care for her beautiful daughter. She and I dined on steak and shared a bottle of bubbly to celebrate my birthday. We spent the evening talking about men and menopause. We shared our stories of hot flashes and supported each other in lowering the temperature of the room to somewhere near freezing. She spoke lovingly of her husband and I confessed my intention to pursue men on the Internet.

I told her that my lovely weekend was to be topped with a date. As fate would have it, my new young suitor happened to be from her hometown. We were tormented as to what to do. Should she drive me back to New York City? Should I come to her house and have my date in a small town? The planning was elaborate. How would I get home? What if this date was as bad as the first? You would have thought we were teenagers. We decided she would bring me back to her house. I would have my date in her town, come back, and sleep in her spare bedroom if it was late. Alternatively, I'd borrow her car and drive myself home that night. The planning was ridiculous. The main difference between this and seventh grade was that we didn't pass one single note.

My Date with Benjamin

On the day of the date, he called me, and I explained that I had found myself at a friend's house in his hometown. He offered to drive me home and take me out in the city. Without hesitation I agreed. So much for the mad planning of menopausal women.

Frantically, I showered and dressed while having a hot flash. It was August. While my friend is also having hot flashes, her husband is very thin and never hot. He had no understanding of why I was sweating, swelling, yelling, crying, and gasping for breath. I had fifteen minutes to be ready. The solution came in the form of teething rings, left in the freezer from years gone by, placed between and under each breast. I was just beginning to breathe normally when the doorbell rang. My friend and I were paralyzed. Her husband pretended not to notice our over-reaction.

Insisting that my friend stay in the kitchen – I knew her nose would be pressed against the window as I left – I went to answer the door for my mystery date. He was exactly as I had imagined: young, cute, and from what I could tell by his emails, incredibly smart. Stepping out with my most vivacious self, I hopped into his car and nervously talked the entire thirty-minute drive to my apartment in the city.

We say we are going out for a drink. I was sure that wouldn't happen. He was looking to play Benjamin to my Mrs. Robinson, and I was looking for a bit of a tune-up. It had been so long since I had sex that I wondered if it really was like riding a bike. We arrived to my neighborhood and he offered to carry my overnight bag up to the apartment. While it was true my doorman could have taken care of the bag for me, I didn't protest. I invited my Benjamin in for a drink.

We sat on opposite ends of the sofa and sipped scotch. This was the first time in years that I had been alone in a room with a man where business wasn't the issue before us. I had no idea what to say, and I somehow thought the thing to do was dazzle him with my big brain. I may have amazed him with my big brain that night, but I believe my big breasts astounded him even more. We talked for a while, but in what I believe was an effort to shut me up, he soon leaned in to kiss me. I was thrilled that my lips remembered what to do. We fumbled for a while in the living room. He was kissing me and climbing on top of me and all I could think about was the fact that I couldn't remember the last time I had been in that position.

"Can you show me your bedroom?"

"Sure."

I had never been so unsure.

He was a bit nervous and admitted that being with an older woman, a real-life Mrs. Robinson, was a fantasy. My Benjamin may have been just as nervous as I was.

In the blink of an eye he was naked and pulling

me toward the bed. His mouth never left mine as his hands struggled to gain access to my breasts. I pulled my shirt over my head and removed my four-hook bra for him. He smiled gratefully and pushing me back onto the bed, lost himself for a moment between my breasts.

Flipping my skirt up, he pulled off my panties and in seconds was on top and inside of me. A couple of thrusts and he was done.

He had a rocking orgasm followed by embarrassment that he had finished so quickly. He was just too excited about fulfilling his Mrs. Robinson fantasy. I was just glad that I could excite that kind of reaction in a young man.

It was all over very quickly and my world wasn't rocked. That said, it was lovely and if he ever reads this, he should know he was responsible for giving me back a little freedom. My appeal to the other sex had been reestablished in my own mind. I was ready and confident enough to continue.

It's just too bad that we didn't have another go at it. Now I would be able to oblige with a little supporting foundation, emotional and otherwise.

Round Two

I was feeling alive for the first time in years. My mind and body began to awaken. Sexual feelings were rising up regularly, and I began to notice that men actually looked at me as I walked down the street. I felt surer of myself, and my assurance made me even more confident at work. It was as if a door was opening and light was just beginning to break through.

After a few days, the emails started coming in fast and furious. Despite the fact that I was rejecting most of the emails out of hand, I had a running correspondence going on with several men at the same time. I could think of nothing but men. I seemed to have absolutely no control. I could stop drinking coffee and smoking cigarettes, but I could not stop my hormonal surges and urges and constant thoughts about men.

My girlfriends were asking for a flowchart. They couldn't keep everyone straight. I was just giving thanks that the men were all straight and decided to ride this wave of men.

As one sixty-year old man was asking for permission to call me, or if I was not comfortable with that to call him, I got an email from another sixty-year-old. By the time his second email arrived, this new older man apparently had a birthday. His profile now said he was sixty-one. I panicked a bit at crossing the sixty-year mark. I looked at his photo. Either his photo was nearly as old as I was or he was lying about his age. I responded to his email and told him how good he looked for his advanced years.

He admitted he had just turned thirty-one and had lied about his age because of his attraction to older women. Thirty-one seemed to be too young, but sixty-one seemed to be a bit too old. In order to ease my discomfort when discussing him with my girlfriends, I decided to dub him the Faux Sixty-Year Old.

The real issue at hand was whether or not I was on a downward slope to ruin. Was it wrong for me to be considering a date with this very young man? We exchanged some charming emails and moved quickly to chatting online. The first chat session was filled with a bit of personal information, teasing and political discussion, which was always good for me. We agreed to meet for a drink the following evening. I logged off the Internet and wondered what I had done. This one seemed to progress very quickly to the meeting phase, and I was worried that I was about to meet my Mr. Goodbar.

I woke up the next morning all aflutter and spent a good part of the day preparing for the evening. His Internet profile said he was very tall, so I was sure to put on high shoes. The Faux Sixty-Year Old had selected the perfect spot to meet for smart cocktails. There were comfortable chairs and sofas and dim lighting, which was always good for an older gal.

When I arrived, he was waiting at the bar in a navy suit and a baby blue shirt with no tie. His skin was the color of coffee ice cream, and his eyes were green. This beautiful specimen of a man stood to greet me. He kept going until his full six-foot-six frame was before me.

"Hello."

His voice was like honey. He smiled and presented me with a dozen yellow roses. Now perhaps he had done this before and since, but then he explained, "I just knew this shade of yellow would be perfect with your hair."

I was a goner.

Amazingly, he was not only charming but also smart. We talked for hours over smart cocktails and then had a little smooch. The smooch turned into a full-fledged kiss that made my toes curl. If we had been standing at the time of that first kiss, my right foot would have popped up, just like in a Doris Day movie.

His fingers brushed my neck and I tasted the bourbon on his tongue as he kissed me.

"Let's get out of here."

All I could do was follow his lead. He kissed me on the way out of the bar. We stopped walking down the street to kiss. We kissed at the stoplights. He walked me to my door, and we kissed some more. It was an actual make out session, truly a lovely thing. Kissing is seriously underrated. We should all spend some serious time on serious kissing.

Faux Sixty-Year Old went home that night with nothing but kisses. He left me breathless. I stayed awake just thinking about his kisses. The next day, I could think of nothing but his mouth. We agreed to meet again that Thursday. I planned to cook and selected a dish that would be fine the next day with friends should he arrive and either one or both of us discovered we had made a horrible error in judgment.

He did come that Thursday. A little initial nervousness passed with a lovely conversation. I am a consummate cook, but I was nervous as he watched me prepare the simple meal I had planned. I roasted fresh asparagus and sliced vine-ripened tomatoes to accompany the perfectly roasted chicken I had placed on the counter to rest. Too nervous to carve, I offered Faux Sixty-Year Old the knife and brushed up against him as I place an apron over his head.

After dinner, we took our wine glasses to the living room and put on a little Etta James. He started with slow kisses and then pulled me closer to him.

His powerful embrace held me up as I melted beneath his touch. He looked into my eyes as his finger traced the curve of my lower lip and chin to my cleavage. He kissed my neck as his hands moved to unbutton my blouse. I didn't protest as he unhooked my bra and then took my nipple into his mouth.

"Take me to your bed."

I willingly obliged, leading the way and leaving a trail of clothes in our wake. His youth and eagerness nearly overwhelmed me. His brown skin looked lovely against my white sheets and even lovelier against my own white skin. We had sex for hours, easily changing positions as if it were a choreographed dance. His strong body pushed my body to its limits. I couldn't remember the last time my legs had been so far apart. I certainly couldn't remember the last time something that large had been between them. While we did take short breaks for food and a brief walk to purchase more condoms, he was my menopausal male muse until he left on Sunday, four days later.

The following day I began to research yoga classes in the city.

Patience

Then came the waiting. I had not had enough of the Faux Sixty-Year Old and I wasn't sure I ever would. I was a woman possessed. Days passed.

In the meantime, I had to do something, so I wrote back to a new man, the Museum Guy. We exchanged a few emails. His picture looked very cute and he always replied with emails that made me laugh. We agreed to meet for a museum date to look at dinosaur bones. One of my favorite places in the world is the American Museum of Natural History in New York City. Even if he were all wrong, I'd still have the tyrannosaurus rex.

Traffic was light so I arrived at the museum early. The day was spectacular so I found a spot out front and opened my book. Of course, at that precise moment, my cell phone rang. It was my mother calling. While I was on the phone with my mother, he arrived. I smiled at him and said good-bye to my mom. I couldn't possibly tell her I had to go because my date had arrived.

"No, I don't really know him."

"Well, I'm not really sure what he does for a

living."

"He's actually much younger than I am."

These are points best left unsaid when talking to one's mother. Instead, I chose to lie to her and say I must run off to a work-related appointment.

Museum Guy was standing there in front of me, and he was actually much cuter than his profile photo. Unlike the disastrous first date, his ass was not the size of Iowa and very cute indeed. I thought that things were looking up. It seemed too good to be true.

As it turned out, the cute face and body was all that there was on the plate. He had the intelligence and the attention span of a gnat. I couldn't believe it. I kept trying. He grew bored of the museum within the hour. I was dismayed. I was so surprised that I agreed to go for a walk in the park. He was at least ten years younger, but he grew weary from our seven-block stroll. We sat on a park bench and attempted conversation.

Empowered by my prior dates, I was comfortable answering any question he lobbed in my direction although he seemed to be refusing to answer any of mine. At first, I thought he was being evasive. Then I suspected he didn't understand them. Mind you, the questions weren't that deep. We're talking first date stuff. Even though I was sure I was speaking in English, it was as if he were hearing some foreign language he didn't understand. I still couldn't believe that someone who could be so funny when he wrote to me could actually not be bright. Perhaps he had a ghostwriter.

I decided to give it one last shot so we went for a bite to eat. Unbelievably, he was that dim. Museum

Guy was a clear example of a nice house with nobody home. He didn't understand. He actually thought I'd let him come to my house to hang out. I felt like I was back in high school.

"No."

"I won't try anything."

"No."

"I can control myself."

"No."

"It must be you who can't control you."

"No."

He leaned over the table and tried to kiss me. All I could do was push him back down and into his chair. Stunned, I went home, a walking nerve ending. Although I could think of nothing but the male form, I couldn't let this man near me, not even for a little good-bye kiss.

I am living proof that the brain is, in fact, a sexual organ that is not to be ignored. Ever!

Boundaries

The Professor was a few years older than I was, and he sent suitably grown-up emails that were clever and charming. He was handsome, and he seemed a bit too good to be true. My friends had all seen the profile photos of the men I have been dating and writing to and all of them gave The Professor the thumbs-up. Even their boyfriends and husbands began to get involved, and all voted for this man.

While his emails were charming, there was an eagerness I now recognize as aggressiveness. During our first conversation, he quickly crossed the line. Now keep in mind that the line is a moving target. It really does depend upon the situation and who is on the other side of it. Certainly, there was more of a sense of raciness in my correspondence with the Faux Sixty-Year-Old, but we both moved to that point gradually, moving the line together during the course of our conversations. This new man suddenly leapt over the line and onto my side. It was almost like a slap in the face. I recoiled, and he quickly backed away, leaving me with the thought that perhaps I had overreacted.

His words kept flashing up on my screen, wondering what happened and asking if I was all right. I simply said goodnight and logged off the site.

The next round of emails came in, and we moved on to instant messaging. It was very late at night, and he quickly became demanding about coming over to my house. Mind you, I have still never met this man and never even heard his voice. I said no, and he became angry. The tone of his messages became abusive.

"How dare you say no to me. Tell me where you live right now. You know all you want is my big dick to suck on."

I couldn't have been more surprised and immediately turned off my computer. This was all new territory for me. I began to doubt myself and thought that perhaps it was the late hour or he had more wine than he should have had before navigating through cyberspace. I decided to express my surprise in an email the next morning. I admit to expecting either silence or an apology. Four days later, he sent a ranting email, explaining what a terrible person I was and saying I was a tease and my goal was to humiliate him.

There is a lesson to be learned here. Always trust your own sense of where your boundaries lie. Trust your boundaries of emotion, space, words and touch. Listen to your inner voice and never waiver. I come back to this particular lesson often. It is one I thought I knew like I know myself but, in fact it is worth repeating regularly to yourself and to everyone you love.

An Embarrassing Moment

More time passed, and the discussions with my fellow menopausal women turned to sex and birth control. There is no way to know when we will menstruate. The fluctuation is extraordinary. Are we ovulating? If one egg makes it and there is one strong swimmer about, are we willing to make the commitment to have a teenager in our retirement? The answer was a resounding no.

So what do we do? Those who are married certainly don't want to turn to condoms with their possibly Viagra-dependant husbands, and those of us who are single don't want to risk reliance on a condom alone. At our age, the Pill doesn't really seem to be an option anymore. We all hate the diaphragm. So where does that leave us? We wistfully remember the sponge.

In the meantime, I am happy to report that Faux Sixty-Year-Old has made contact again. In preparation for our next date, I went online in search of a better means of birth control and discovered that one can still buy contraceptive sponges in Canada, both the sponge I was familiar with and a Canadian version that seemed like an excellent option. I ordered enough of the foreign contraband for my friends and me to try. In anticipation, I decided to have a trial run.

The Canadian version was much smaller than the sponge I had used before. The box was filled with sealed containers that looked like those little packs of grape jelly you get at a diner. Peeling back the foil top, I inspected my contraband before insertion. I needed to be sure that what went up did in fact come down. I am happy to report that I had successful insertion and removal. As several girlfriends were eager to hear the outcome, the calls went out, and there was much joy in the land.

Faux Sixty-Year Old arrived at my door on a Friday night. Knowing what was about to happen, I prepped with a sponge just before his arrival. I opened the door to a young man who seemed bolder and more confident or perhaps my new layer of protection had emboldened me. My encounters with him were boosting my confidence. I felt as comfortable with my sexual self as I ever had.

His six-foot-six frame lifted and moved me into positions I didn't think were possible. Had my leg ever been past my head before? Just as I thought we were done, a surge of energy passed through me, and I threw him back with tremendous force, pinning him to the bed. His strong thirty-one year old body rallied quickly under my touch. In a moment he was hard again and I climbed on top, straddling his body, then sliding down onto his enormous penis. I grabbed his thighs and rode him with such abandon that I surprised myself. He watched me, then cried out as we both came and then collapsed. It was as fast as it was phenomenal.

The next morning, after waiting the designated amount of time for removal, the moment of truth arrived. Would sponge removal be as easy as it had been during the trial run? While it had been some time, I had used this particular form of birth control in the past. I wasn't in completely unfamiliar territory.

I tried everything. I reread the instructions. I was beginning to panic. The brochure said I was to relax. Relax! My trial run hadn't taken into consideration that an extremely large penis would be pushing my contraband sponge much further up than I could have ever done on my own. This is the moment a middle-aged woman who is dating discovers the real need for Valium. I took the Valium and decided to wait. Perhaps a glass of wine would assist. It was useless. I gave up and decided to try again the next morning.

By the time Monday morning arrived, I was in a panic. Now, since I didn't have a regular doctor, I had to call the unknown gynecologist and make an appointment for sponge removal.

"Hello."

"I'd like to make an appointment to see the doctor today."

"You're in luck! The doctor has several appointments available next week."

"Next week!" I was on the verge of tears. "I need to see him today."

Of course, she wanted to know why there was any urgency. By the time the conversation was over, I had explained my story to three different women, including the nurse. Despite their insights on sponge removal and my precarious situation, the staff still wanted to know how I got a hold of the contraband sponges. I promised to bring in a sample sponge for inspection and was finally able to make an appointment for later that day.

I arrived at the doctor's office, and they were respectful. I traveled down the long hallway for my first meeting with the doctor. Apparently, my story had preceded me. He was kind and understanding, and my recently increased libido impressed him. After sponge removal, we discussed hot flashes, hormone replacement therapy, and birth control. As it turned out, at my advanced age, the need for birth control was minor. He suggested that, in my current menopausal state, using nothing put me at about the same risk of pregnancy that I had in my twenties while I used the Pill. By adding spermicidal, it became a no-brainer. Adding a condom to that, it would take an Immaculate Conception.

The Next Step

I didn't know what the next step was, but I was overwhelming myself. I felt ready for a real relationship. Mind you, I wasn't exactly sure what that actually meant either. After living alone for so long, I didn't know if I wanted someone else constantly in my life or if I was really just looking for a part-time lover to come and see me when I decided the time was right.

For the first time in my life, I felt I wanted to share my life with someone. I wanted to be in the presence of someone who knew my secrets, flaws, and sorrows. I wanted someone who loved me not only in spite of those things but also because of them. I felt as if there was a gaping hole in the center of my being that needed filling. That hole was probably always there. I had just been afraid to acknowledge it. Menopause was allowing me to take stock, to get to know myself a little better.

Women spend years making secrets and a lifetime keeping them. The secrets become so protected, that we often are guilty of keeping the truth from ourselves. I feel afraid to examine myself too carefully, for fear of what I might find. Feeling open and vulnerable has always scared me. Interestingly, I discovered that once I was willing to recognize that I needed someone else, I was happier with myself yet somehow lonelier at the same time. It's a horrible thing to admit. I was lonely. I'd never minded being alone. In fact, I rather enjoyed it. But I wanted to take care of someone.

I think women are by nature caregivers. Even those of us who live alone often put aside our own needs and desires to make sure others are happy. We are somehow happy knowing that someone else's needs are taken care of to the detriment of ourselves. The difference in how I felt now was that I was willing to allow someone to take care of me as well.

Hormones were drudging up deep feelings and I began to cry every day. When I was growing up, I learned the distinction between real tears, real sorrow, and the tears I would use to get what I wanted. In my family, they were called "crocodile tears." Was I filled with crocodile tears, or was I suffering from some kind of loss? This reverse puberty was overwhelming and self-consuming. I began to feel desperate, and I made more calls to take a pulse about how others were feeling. The truth was, for the first time I was calling friends to try to tell them how I was feeling.

My new cries for help were unprecedented. In the past, my phone had been the one ringing with the needy voice on the other end. My friends were taken aback. I knew they wanted to be willing participants, but the change in roles was hard for them as well. It didn't matter. I still had my feelings hurt.

It wasn't just about hot flashes. This time of life, this change, had me crying at least once a day. There was no specific reason or rationale. It just was. I was worried about everything. I felt sorry for myself. World events moved me deeply. Any kind of human kindness touched me.

Despite all precautions, I had an irrational fear about being pregnant. I cried as I awaited the results of regular over-the-counter pregnancy tests.

I cried when I was sad, and I cried when I was happy.

I cried at compassion, and I cried at brutality.

I cried when I tried to explain how I was feeling.

I cried because no one understood me.

I cried because I worried about my mother.

I cried because I worried I was becoming my mother.

I cried because I worried about money.

I cried because I was so lucky to have the most fantastic friends you could possibly imagine.

I am crying now. There is no end to my tears.

The real problem was that my hormones were still running amok. I still thought about men constantly. I thought about sex at least once an hour.

A woman's need for sex, and lots of it, is just not discussed enough, not in any book about menopause or conversations between women about sex. The female libido is a funny thing, and it seems that mine is up for almost any joke.

Tall or short.

Young or old.

Bald, dark, or gray.

It didn't seem to matter. Any one thing or combination of the above clearly had potential to amuse, so I was open-minded about what the vision of the elusive perfect man was for me.

Another Round of Men

Internet dating seems to go in waves. You have a little bit of downtime, and then more email begins to arrive out of nowhere. If you're lucky, you've got a little left over from prior waves to keep you going.

Keeping in mind that I believed I was now ready for a relationship, two seemingly age-appropriate men, both younger but in their forties, came calling. They were very similar. Both lived outside of the city. Both were divorced and had children. The first one was quick to move. His Internet profile was very complete, and there was more than one photo. We exchanged a couple of emails and arranged to meet for lunch. There were no chat sessions. He simply asked me out for lunch. It was quite a refreshing change and seemed somehow very old-fashioned.

The day of our pending date arrived. He sent me a note saying how excited he was to meet me. It felt quite promising. Just a couple hours before we were to meet, he called me up. He was breathless and said he had to cancel. A child-related emergency had come up. He apologized profusely. We exchanged a couple more emails, but nothing ever came of it. We never arranged another date, and I'll never know why.

In the meantime, I was exchanging email with the other age-appropriate gentleman. He was handsome and articulate. His emails were very funny, and we seemed to have quite a bit of chemistry happening. Of course, email wasn't everything, as I learned from the Museum Guy with a ghost writer. I found myself quizzing this new man, and he was quick to respond. Enough tests. We decided to meet for drinks after work.

With several dates under my belt, I was now able to dress myself. I considered it to be quite an achievement. In spite of being able to dress, I was so nervous about meeting this new man that I was one big hot flash.

The chill of fall was in the air, and I was sweating on my way to the restaurant as if it were August. As I shed every layer that I could on my way to meet him, I was thrilled to run into a girlfriend on the street who dutifully gave me an appropriate pep talk and made light of my sweaty situation.

I arrived at the restaurant a couple minutes early, so I bellied up to the bar. I looked great, and I was having a good hair day. With a lovely location, fantastic music, a single malt scotch, and a handsome man, I could have been a happy woman.

My date arrived, and I was pleasantly pleased. He was handsome, charming, talkative, and open about himself. He told great stories about his family and his business. It should have been a perfect first date. We both tried quite valiantly but, even with scotch added, it was clear that there would never be a second date.

Simply put, there is just no way to gauge

chemistry between two human beings in cyberspace. Face to face is the only way to do it. Even when it seems as if the planets are aligned, a date is sometimes nothing more than a date.

While this third round of dating was very disappointing, all was not lost. Faux Sixty-Year Old resurfaced to join the roster. I was incredibly happy to hear from him. During this period, he made contact on several occasions, and I was delighted.

I found myself thinking of him day and night. Sex with the Faux Sixty-Year Old was like a drug. I couldn't get enough of him. I loved running my hands along his muscled arms and chest as he entered me; watching his green eyes watching me; seeing my white thighs squeeze into his brown ribs as we both came. My short white body looked petite and feminine against his massive six-foot-six brown frame. He could lift me, flip me, and turn me upside down with the flick of a wrist. I felt like a ballerina, my toes pointing gracefully to the sky as he pushed every muscle in my body to its limit. Even when he was inside of me, his hands could reach every inch of my body from stem to stern. Sex with Faux Sixty-Year Old released my inner goddess. I was the sexiest woman alive.

I didn't want to be, but I was smitten. I truly enjoyed his company, even when we weren't having earth-shattering, aerobic sex. He couldn't have been more inappropriate, unrealistic, or wrong for me. Even worse, each time he left, I realized I actually missed him. I couldn't deny that it was true. The encounters were more than fun, but his youth was beginning to annoy me, especially how he communicated, only via email. The menopausal synapses finally connected, and I realized he had all of my contact information, but I had none of his. Not everyone spent his or her life on the Internet. I was sure other women were receiving yellow roses, but he needed lessons in common communication courtesy. Despite that, I was eager to have him entertain me.

I tried to explore why I felt the way I did. I convinced my friends and myself that it was his physical power and beauty and nothing more. I began to resent that he was charming and smart, and I was angry he wasn't more available to me. Once again, we get to what has defined my relationships, doing things my way and doing what I want.

So, what do I want?

Lack of Focus

A lull occurred in the action and I finally realized that something else was afoot. My raging hormones seemed to be impacting my ability to multitask. I am a smart woman who used to make my living multitasking. I excelled at it. But, for the moment, not only was my ability to multitask compromised, but I didn't even seem to be able to focus on one thing at a time. Perhaps it was my preoccupation with the opposite sex. When you think about men all the time, crossing the street can be a dangerous thing.

I discovered that merely talking about sex and other hormonal issues could release me and allow me to do something else for a brief period. I talked to anyone who would listen. Everyone around me, whether they knew me or not, was aware of the progress of each and every hot flash. I was calling on both male and female friends to talk about men. I felt incredibly juvenile, but, as a result I was able to function in the world as an adult. I couldn't lose sight of the fact that not only was I having hot flashes, crying, laughing, and attempting to date the male portion of the Eastern seaboard, but I was also attempting to make a go at a new career. It was hard to date and make a living at the same time.

As more time passed, I discovered that I actually did work for a living. I tried to lose myself in work and got down to the business of paying my mortgage. What else could I do?

There had been no word from Faux Sixty-Year Old, and I was growing restless. I needed a distraction in the form of a man. The next wave of email finally began to come in. Again, I rejected most of the advances immediately. By this time, I was getting bolder, so I decided it was time to attempt to send out some of the initial communications.

The shoe was now on the other foot. I was being rejected. While the rejections were quite a blow to the ego, it was more troubling to get no response at all. Did they never see it? Was I not even worthy of any kind of response? Should I cry about it? Should I feel remorse for men I have treated in the same way? These responses or lack thereof should have shaped my Internet dating etiquette from that moment on. Unless the suitor was an absolute nut job, a polite "No, thank you" or "I'm otherwise engaged" was the right thing to do. It only took a second to do. If that same man got up the nerve to approach in person, I would certainly, at a minimum, say "No, thank you" rather than walk away as if he had never appeared before me and spoke.

Because of the initial effort coming from both sides, I believed this round of dating would be more diverse. Mind you, the diversity didn't so much make this new round of dating any better, but it did make it plentiful. Once again, a flowchart seemed necessary.

Not only were there new men in this round, but a few from prior rounds were still making contact. Perhaps I could multitask after all!

The first in this round was Mr. Brooklyn. A grown man in his fifties, he had been born and bred in Brooklyn. His emails quizzed me as I had quizzed others, so I figured he was on the cautious side. His photos were suspect, a little grainy and a little out of focus, but he seemed like a very nice man. I decided the grown-up decision to meet an adult for coffee for a real conversation was a sensible thing to do. It was time to judge a book by what was written inside, not by its cover. We met for coffee, and neither of us was at a loss for words. We seemed to agree on social and political issues. But we just didn't like each other. It wasn't just a lack of chemistry. If we had met at a party, we wouldn't have spoken. I couldn't even see him at a party with any of my friends. We had absolutely nothing in common.

Next in the lineup was the Financial Consultant. He was tall, blond, and handsome. I am not usually attracted to balding blonds, but something about this man made me want to meet him. Quite simply, he made me laugh. We agreed to meet for lunch, and he selected a lovely place near his office. He was very charming. We spoke easily about life and loves past, and we had a lovely time. He was a bit flirtatious, and so was I. He suggested getting together again, and we exchanged emails to that effect. His emails were even a bit on the sexy side now. I didn't really mind. His work got busy, and the holidays were approaching. His emails became work confessionals rather than love notes.

Perhaps he was having his own midlife crisis, so I offered to take him to lunch. On the day we were to meet, he called to cancel because of work. I understood. I had been there myself. I had buried myself in my last job. I had no interest in being buried in someone else's job. I had further holiday greetings from him, but there were no real overtures. I didn't shed any crocodile tears over this one, but I wouldn't have minded if he called again.

My Oedi-pal

Faux Sixty-Year Old man reappeared for a brief yet lovely encounter and was a welcome addition to my humdrum days. He was as attentive as ever and his beautiful brown body made me enjoy my own body as he did. I knew he'd fade away again, so the time was right to consider the idea of another young suitor.

I received a very flirtatious email from a very cute, young man. The Web site he was on gave age ranges, not specific ages. I found this infuriating because I now found myself in the older checkbox. Despite my checkbox, he still sought me out. From his photos, I had no idea how old he could possibly be. In one photo, he was with a very small child. I asked if he was divorced and if that was perhaps his daughter. He informed me that his father, who was probably a better age for me, had remarried. The little girl was, in fact, his sister. The modern American family.

I agreed to meet this younger man for a drink. Foolishly, I decided to meet him at one of my favorite haunts. He arrived, and he was better looking than his photo. We had more drinks than what is advised for a first date, but the conversation flowed quite easily, and

I was having fun.

I pulled together all of my courage and asked the big question, "What the hell are you doing flirting with and going out with someone old enough to be your mother?"

A very sly grin came across his face, and he suddenly seemed shy. With much goading, he finally confessed.

"My last affair was with an older woman."

"Really? How much older?"

"Probably about your age."

"Really?"

"I learned a lot," he boasted.

"Really?"

"She was my best friend's mother."

"What? What did your friend have to say about that?"

"He never knew."

"Is he still your friend?"

"Sure."

This was a bit salacious, even for me. It seemed beyond Mrs. Robinson. Even so, my mind immediately fell upon the name I would use when it came to discussions with my friends. He would now and forever be dubbed as my Oedi-pal.

My mind was back in the moment and I noticed my third scotch sitting before me. Never have too many smart cocktails at your favorite bar with a very attractive and very young man. One thing led to another, and I let him kiss me at the bar. It wasn't creepy. I don't think that anyone thought we should have gotten a room. It was just a little smooch. I clearly had had my fill of scotch. It was time to go.

The weather was still lovely, so we sat briefly on the bench just outside the restaurant while he smoked a cigarette. The bench was just in front of the window. We could see inside the bar we had just left. The next thing I knew, he was kissing me. It was one of those wacky make-out kisses you have when you're first dating. Now I knew this was wildly inappropriate, especially considering the location, but it felt great and when you reach a certain age, as long as you're not hurting yourself or anyone else, I think you should just be able to do whatever feels great. So we sat on the bench for about fifteen minutes and just kissed. I finally had the good sense to stop and to tell him to go home. I then poured myself into a cab.

The next morning I called all of my girlfriends and they were scandalized by my behavior and by his tender age of 30. This whole Mrs. Robinson fantasy was fascinating. This was my third earnest suitor who was truly interested in a much older woman. While I was more than happy for their preference for older women, I was more than baffled by it as well. I began to survey men of all ages on the issue and typically got a shrug in response.

I did get one answer that I think is worth sharing. The man is a smart, handsome, thirty-six-year old. He is married with children, and he is gainfully employed. He is an all-around nice guy who openly admits he has never dated an older woman. That being said, I think his theory is a good one.

He suggested that as we move through life, the benchmarks that society places before us are obvious. When a woman is between twenty-five and thirty, if she is not already married, marriage is often the main goal, the driving force in her life. Then the biological clock starts ticking away. The years between thirty and forty are crucial for making headway in this department. We don't just think about having children, but our friends and family assault us on all fronts. We wonder if we can fulfill our destiny as women.

Both my theorist and I made the assumption that men actually want to date women and not girls, leaving out the under twenty-five group. My friend explained that the clear safety zone for dating falls above forty-four years old. He further explained that women over forty-four are moving too quickly toward menopause for children and have a whole different set of requirements for what is expected in a mate. I think he's right. We no longer apply the baby-making pressure to the equation and so the desire for an older woman grows in the younger man.

More Hot Flashes

I seemed to have a little more downtime than usual. It wasn't just me. Everyone was spending less time on personal matters and turning all attention to politics and the war. It seemed as if my hot flashes were running as hot as the political debates. The hot flashes were never-ending. I wasn't sleeping as well as usual. I woke myself up in the middle of the night because I was wildly ripping the clothes off my body. I was alone and hotter than hell. It was unbelievable. I was finally comfortable. I'd drift back off to sleep, but I'd awaken because I was so cold that I had to get up to retrieve the duvet from the floor. Months of practice enabled me to strip and merely throw the comforter to the side for easy recovery interrupting my sleep a bit less.

A few girlfriends were considering hormone replacement therapy to subside their hot flashes. Others were talking about herbal teas and tincture of sage. I wasn't ready to go there yet. While I was occasionally uncomfortable, I remained unconcerned by the changes happening in my body.

In spite of all that was going on, my libido was

higher than ever. As a result, my gynecologist said that, unless I was too uncomfortable or having trouble coping with the changes that were happening that I shouldn't, "screw with a good thing."

I applauded his turn of a phrase and I happened to agree with him. I might change my mind in the next six months, but for the moment, I preferred to focus on the thing that made my hot flashes disappear. Sex.

Even just thinking about sex made my hot flashes subside. The real problem was where I could find sex. Despite the fact I had a couple encounters over the last few months, what I really wanted was something on a more regular basis. I hadn't yet met a man who I thought was worthy of relationship status.

My hot flashes now dictated how I dressed. I had to rethink how I dressed for everyday life. After much discussion with girlfriends over issues relating to fashion, we decided that none of it mattered. Damn fashion. Layers were the only answer. All that matters was that we could dress in layers. Layers enabled us to change clothes throughout the day as often as our temperature dictated. Even the changing season and temperature drops offered no relief. What new hell was I living this winter to be hot and cold at the same time?

The Chef

During this time of severe flashing, I began a correspondence with a charming man. He told me about his recent career path. He claimed to have started his own technology business and said he was pursuing a career as a chef at the same time. We discussed our shared love of cooking, and he sent me some of the menus from the cookbook he was working on. I was enjoying his willingness to share.

We corresponded every day. These were not typical emails. They were honest-to-goodness letters. He told me that he was on the road for business, and I looked forward to his daily explanations of head and heart. I don't use the term often, who does, but I confess I was – enchanted. He told me his tales of childhood and discussed his relationships with his mother and closest friends. We seemed in tune, and I responded with stories about myself.

With each letter I felt I was learning more and more about the Chef, including his family, friends, travel, business, childhood, and hopes and dreams. I eagerly awaited my daily communication. It took a month of daily correspondence before he began to move toward that invisible line. The flirting began in earnest, but other tales were mingled in. Was he testing boundaries after such a prolonged courtship? Was this actually a courtship? Certainly, he was sharing more information than any other man I had met so far, online or in person.

The Chef drew his line in the sand and then crossed it. He finally confessed. He admitted to a love of erotica. You'd think that this might send up a red flag or two, but he had taken so long to draw the line in the sand that I wasn't sure why such a minor thing required a confession. I knew he was a nice Catholic boy, but this was certainly not such a sin. Clearly, with the intent to shock and with a preface of "I must warn you," he shared some favorite photos. More than anything else, they were sweet in nature. They were like pinup girls from the forties or fifties. There was nothing shocking or salacious about them. He seemed quite shy about his new confession. My response was to somehow offer my cyber support. Did he think I would be shocked? In truth, I found his confession to be incredibly charming. My shocked reaction was to stop writing and suggest actually meeting him for a smart cocktail.

What happened next was the surprise. While the Chef seemed happy sharing intimate details of his life over the Internet, he had absolutely no interest in actually meeting. Wasn't that the whole point of internet dating, to actually meet? All I could do was wonder: Was anything he said actually true? Was he really a chef? Was he really traveling, or was he just sitting in his room somewhere, afraid to ever come out?

The simple fact of the matter is that you can never tell a person's real intentions when the talking is done without human contact and in complete anonymity. Don't allow yourself to be swept in without some kind of actual human contact. Even a phone call could make all the difference. My Chef was a complete waste of time.

Round Five

I was spending more time on the Internet and at home watching the news. I wasn't sure if it was my hormones or what was going on in the world, but, each time I turned on the news, I burst into tears. As I felt myself falling into deep despair, Faux Sixty-Year Old resurfaced one last time to help kick off a new round of dating. I happily invited him over for a little consolation. Within minutes of his arrival we were naked. I loved how this beautiful young hard-bodied man looked in my bed. I had a lovely time as he threw me from one end of the bed to the other, as if I were a feather, repeating our familiar lusty dance. The sex was good, but somehow the passion was gone and we ended up chatting in the living room over a glass of wine about life and politics. He asked to borrow one of my books which he promised to return soon.

"Can I come over tomorrow and cook for you?" he asked.

"I'd love that!"

I was stunned. I expected that this encounter would be more of a last hurrah.

"Great," he said.

"I'd love to have you cook for me, but I'm not in the mood for disappointment."

"What do you mean?"

"It's been ages since I've seen you and I don't want to count on you coming with dinner if you're not..."

"I'll be here." He interrupted. "I've missed you. It will be fun."

With one last warning, I looked at him and stressed the importance of actually following through.

"Don't say it unless you mean it," I said.

I told him that, if something or anything came up to change his plans, he wasn't to send me an email.

"Call me," I said. "I am not tethered to my computer."

I could not have been clearer. As he departed, he told me that nothing could possibly happen that would make him change his plans.

"I'll be there. I promise."

I was busy the next day at work. I had no messages from the Faux Sixty Year-Old. I decided to check my email before heading home, and there were no messages there. I felt like a schoolgirl and hurried home to meet my date.

It was getting late, and I hadn't heard from him. He never did show up. Instead, he sent an email long after he was to arrive saying he couldn't make it. Livid, I wrote back, letting him know that I would not tolerate being treated in that fashion. The next morning he wrote back, attempting to make his case. As much as I'd like to see him again, I had enough. I simply wrote back a one-word response.

"No."

I was done, so next on the roster was the Long Island Dad, an age-appropriate, divorced man from Europe who was living in Long Island with his children. We exchanged several emails and decided to meet for lunch at a French bistro. He spent a lot of time selecting a place, and he was careful to be sure that he accommodated me in every way. The day we agreed to meet, it was raining cats and dogs. In translation, it was a very bad hair day for me. I arrived. He had already arranged for our table to be set, and he had reviewed the wine list. We had a glass of wine at the bar and moved to the table for our meal. We talked for hours, and he told me about his children and his divorce. I learned about his siblings and his parents. We had too much wine. Our lunch had gone on for nearly five hours when he drove me home. He gave me a little peck as we said goodnight. I had a very nice time. It wasn't a stellar time, but we had fun. I confess that I expected there would be a second date. He asked me to call him, and the next day I left a message to thank him for the lovely afternoon.

I never heard from him again. I confess that it's quite mysterious to me. I'll never get the chance, but I'd love to know why he decided to make no further contact. My guess is that he was married.

Human Contact

While all of this Internet madness had been going on, I found myself confronted by actual human contact. I had met someone in person who was flirting with me, and I was flirting back. This was an experience I hadn't had for years, and I wasn't sure about the protocol. An age-appropriate man was smiling, flirting, and telling stories. I was finding him to be incredibly sexy. We had actually known each other for a while. He was a bartender at one of my favorite haunts, and he had seen me at my best and my worst. I flirted back and talked to my friends about how cute I thought he was. Not all of them agreed, but none could disagree with how incredibly straight he was.

Over the course of time, I believed I heard him discuss a girlfriend. Someone else said he thought The Bartender may actually be living with her. I was more than disappointed. I decided to put thoughts of him aside, despite his continued flirtation. Flirting was harmless enough, and the male attention definitely made me happy. I was content seeing him at his work on occasion and not giving him another thought.

On one particular evening, I stopped by his bar for a smart cocktail with a friend from work. The Bartender was getting off work, so he stopped by to say good-bye. Since we were friends, he moved in for a kiss. My natural response was to smile and extend my cheek. He obligingly kissed it. Then he moved in and laid one on my lips. Very softly. Very sweetly. Very surprisingly. The gay man with me wondered who the fool was that had acted so inappropriately. I had no response, and I am seldom speechless.

I was confused. I called everyone to discuss it. Maybe he wasn't living with someone. He was clearly interested, and the feeling was mutual.

I decided to wait for at least a week before I put myself in a position to see him again. I arrived, and he told me how beautiful I looked. I smiled. He took my hand and kissed it. I smiled. Before the evening was over, he said he wanted to call me and tell me his story.

Could it be that I was actually going to date someone who hadn't materialized out of cyberspace? I gave him my number, and he left two messages before we made actual contact. He called to let me know that he was sorry he missed me, but he was leaving town. He said he'd call as soon as he got back in a couple days. He didn't disappoint. The phone rang, and he was there, whispering sweet nothings and saying how beautiful I was, how much he cared for me, and how he was living with someone but found me so irresistible that he absolutely couldn't help himself.

I immediately began to rationalize. This was New York. Living with someone could mean many things. Just the mere fact of how difficult it is to find an apartment drives people to live together after divorce. Living with someone could mean nothing.

So I asked, "Are you living with this woman, or are you actually living with her? Like being married?"

He could have lied. He could have said anything. I gave him the perfect out. He placed great importance on telling me the truth, even though he was about to lie to the woman he lived with. He could have said nothing and invited me for a smart cocktail. I would have left with no questions asked. But now it was out there, and I asked the question.

"It's like being married, just without the gifts."

Both of us were disappointed. But now we were both clear about the situation and said good-bye.

I could think of nothing but him for days.

'Tis the Season

The holidays were approaching, and other men from cyberspace were calling, looking for someone to decorate their tree. An age-appropriate teacher who lived in Queens began to send email, and he was eager to make contact. His subscription to the dating service he was using was running out. He asked me to write to him at his personal email address. This means he would know mine. The Teacher seemed normal enough, so the only red flag was the fact that he lived in Queens. Again, I had to consider whether I could travel outside of Manhattan or not to see a man.

The Teacher seemed shy and sweet. We exchanged several emails. Then he unexpectedly sent me a note, telling me that he was actually seeing someone else and wished me luck in my quest for a man.

"After all," he said, "I don't double-dip."

His comment disgusted me. Were women dips at a hors d'oeuvre table at a Christmas party? Clearly, this one was no great loss.

As I sat there stunned and staring at my computer screen, a mystery man, another younger man, sent a request for an instant messaging session. He was thirty-one years old. He was exotic and handsome. He was Moroccan. He knows he was beautiful. He had posted multiple photos on the Web site. I accepted his invitation to chat.

During this chat session, he sent additional stunning photos. I was amazed he wanted to meet. I agreed to meet this handsome Moroccan for a drink the following day. He selected a modest place for a smart cocktail. He arrived, and he was lovely and charming. We had both arranged to be somewhere else after a two-hour window so our date was brief. The Moroccan asked if he could see me again. I said yes, and we picked a date.

In anticipation of date day, the Moroccan sent several emails and caught me online a couple times, promptly sending instant messages. He had been thinking about our date, and he wanted to cook for me. He thought I should taste one of his traditional Moroccan dishes. He was inspired because his sister was visiting from home. He told me about his days with his sister and shared photos of the two of them together. His sister was beautiful. Their parents must have been stunning as well.

I had been incredibly busy at work. I wrapped up a few things in the office, and I arrived home to prepare for his arrival. He was late. Suddenly realizing his incredible youth and remembering what happened with the Faux Sixty-Year Old, I checked my email. The Moroccon wasn't coming. He found our differences, which I assumed to be age, too great. I was beside myself. I should have been angry, but, as a hormonal surge coursed through my body, tears leapt to my eyes. I had a good cry, and I felt sorry for myself for the rest of the evening.

Oedi-pal continued to write and call, leaving messages and asking me to call him. Remembering the bench incident and being mindful that the incident actually took place outside the bar where the sexy bartender worked, I had avoided any further contact with my Oedi-pal.

One night, I was out with a friend for an after-theater drink to discuss the show. As we were enjoying our smart cocktails, another friend called from across town. He had been out having too much holiday cheer, and, since we were neighbors, we discussed sharing a cab home. In anticipation of my friend's call, I didn't put on my reading glasses to check who was on the other end of my vibrating phone. My phone danced across the bar. I grabbed it and flipped it open. To my surprise, it was Oedi-pal. After some initial stammering, I promised to call him back. I knew I shouldn't be having a conversation with him with even one drop of scotch in my system.

The next morning, I returned his call. He wondered what I had been up to since he had left so many messages. I agreed to meet him. After all, he was a sweet young man, despite his affair with his best friend's mother. I had had enough with my recent foiled attempts with Faux Sixty-Year Old and the Moroccan and this young man was trying desperately to spend some time with me.

I had been invited to a holiday party. I didn't invite my Oedi-pal to join me, but instead told him to make the trip to my apartment, which was at least an hour-long commute for him. I said I'd see him late and he obliged.

I couldn't believe I had summoned this young man to my house for no other reason than to have my way with him. I was at the party when my phone rang announcing that Oedi-pal had arrived in my neighborhood. I met him on the corner, and we walked to my apartment. It apparently had taken more than an hour for his commute, and he wondered if he was still truly in New York City. I took him home and cut to the chase. My body was longing for sex, but there was no way Oedi-pal would be able to measure up to the six-foot-six man who had preceded him in my bedroom.

For the first time I was calling the shots. I offered him a drink, turned on some music and then really looked at him. Oedi-pal was handsome, with a full head of dark hair and a lovely mouth. He smiled impishly as I looked him over and pushed his glasses back up on his nose.

"What? Is something wrong?"

"Nothing's wrong."

I walked over to him, took the drink from his hand and kissing him, straddled his lap. I pulled off my sweater and then took off his glasses. I could feel him getting excited beneath me and shifted my body to egg him on.

I enjoyed the feeling of being in charge. I led him to my bedroom and demanded, "Take off your clothes."

He happily obliged and eagerly awaited further instruction. I just wanted to have sex; I didn't have a lesson plan. This was clearly a bad decision on my part.

I did my best to instruct him.

"Kiss me here."

"Touch me there."

"Oh, please fuck me."

"Oooo baby. I want you."

My heart wasn't in it. In fact, I could have done a better job by myself. He however was smitten.

Here's the lesson learned. Even when hormonal surges and urges seem to have the best of you, your brain should always be the controlling sex organ. Perhaps this is a real difference in men and women, but, for me, sex for the sake of sex is rarely worth it.

I discussed this incident at length with my fellow menopausal friends. I didn't even think this was worth crying about. How could this possibly be? Perhaps I was coming out on the other end. My Oedi-pal continued to call and I continued to leave his messages unanswered.

Indiscretions

I needed a break from the Internet, so I went back to work.

A friend suggested we meet for a smart cocktail at The Bartender's bar. Surely it had been long enough since we had last spoken about the inappropriateness of our seeing each other. I was an adult. Why not?

He greeted me, "Hello, beautiful." Then he kissed me on the cheek.

The Bartender was more than attentive, and so was I. I was feeling bold about flirting with someone who found me as charming as I thought I could be. The next morning, he called. He told me about his plans for New Year's Eve and asked when he could see me. He was away with his girlfriend.

I kept repeating to myself, "*You are the other woman. You are the other woman.*"

He called me a couple times when he was gone. He told me he was returning on Sunday night.

He asked, "What time can you see me on Monday?"

I paused, but it was only long enough to have enough breath to say, "How about five o'clock?"

On Monday, I had a busy day. I came home in time for his arrival. The Bartender was a bit late, but he made up for it by arriving with flowers and a bottle of wine. He cleaned up well and was looking very handsome. I offered him a drink and we had a lovely adult conversation. We discussed life, loves, and family. Then he kissed me. It was nice to be kissed by a grown man.

I was taken with him. The animal attraction was undeniable. I don't remember ever having such an animal attraction to anyone. We devoured each other. The evening is a blur, like a film flickering by too quickly.

His hands on my body. The taste of his skin and the cries as we came together. Exhausted we dress so he could go home. I tried to be nonchalant as he kissed me goodbye, but the moment our bodies touched again we nearly ignited. Once again we were ripping at each other, clothes falling away as we fell to the living room floor for one more delicious moment of ecstasy.

Pure, unadulterated sex could be quite refreshing with an adult.

The thought of The Bartender finding me irresistible made me smile. He was gone for ten minutes before he called to say he missed me.

The Bartender

My thoughts for the next few days were about nothing but The Bartender: his eyes, his voice, his taste, and his smell. I remembered how his hands felt on my body.

He called me daily. Despite the fact that I shouldn't lose sight of the reality that I was the other woman, I made plans to see him again.

He came at noon. In deference to his lapsed Catholicism, I greeted him at the door wearing nothing but black patent heels, which were enough to spur three hours of lovemaking before we showered so he could go to work.

That very evening, a friend wanted to meet for a smart cocktail at The Bartender's bar. My friend didn't know what I had been up to, and I had more fun than expected while I watched him work behind the bar. I thought naughty thoughts about what those hands had been doing just a short time before. My friend and I left the bar quite late and quite drunk. As a result, I got little sleep. I woke up, smelled The Bartender on my sheets, and realized that I shouldn't call him. I took my bubble bath and thought of him.

The Bartender called on his way back to work.

"I love your body and think about how I'd like to try and count all of your freckles."

"I'd like to let you try," I teased. "You wear me out. I'm exhausted."

"I could nap for days in your arms, but tonight I have to go to work."

The conversation was short but sweet. I resisted the desire to go watch him work.

Another Round

New Year's Eve came and went quietly this year. I resolved to perform a random act of kindness each day. I realized how special I felt when a complete stranger said I looked great or when someone did something as simple as holding open a door. I cried while remembering moments. The crying continued.

I cried because I was alone.

I cried because I had to take down my Christmas tree.

I cried because I loved the way Etta James sang, "A Sunday Kind of Love." That's what I needed, a Sunday kind of love. I wondered if I'd ever find that, and I cried more. I cried because I wanted The Bartender but resolved to look for an available man.

I went out for a couple of New Year's Day parties and met quite a few new people. I had a fantastic time, and I was sure this was how I should start off a new year. But I didn't meet one man who was both single and straight. I went home and turned on my computer. Several emails were waiting.

The first to appear on the horizon was a very handsome man in his fifties. We only exchanged one round of emails. Group Sex Guy made it very clear that he was looking for someone who also found other women attractive. He was only looking for a sexual relationship, and each encounter would be a party. I didn't think I needed to say anything else. I simply said, "No, thank you." I will say that I applaud his honesty. He knew exactly what he was looking for and delivered the message clearly. I, for one, was glad I found out before any time was wasted.

At the same time, I was getting email from a couple of men who I thought would be better served by meeting each other rather than me. The Shrink gave good initial email, so I shared my number with him. The initial telephone conversation was probing. He asked many questions, but he didn't really believe any of my answers. I felt like he was calling me a liar. On the other hand, the Needy Photographer couldn't get enough. I could have told him anything, and he would have believed me.

"Well, actually, my parents were aliens."

"I was dropped off on Planet Earth forty-eight years ago."

"I'm actually eight hundred and sixteen years old."

The Needy Photographer was more than eager to meet me. I said I'd meet him for coffee, but my work was getting busy and his schedule seemed just as crazy as mine. We just couldn't seem to make it happen. I felt as if I were a victim of cyberstalking. Every time I went online, he was there. I couldn't check email without at least one message from him being there. While I was reading my emails, the Needy Photographer was sending an instant message. I told him I'd call him if I got a chance before he left town. He told me he was a one-woman man. Not surprisingly, I didn't seem to find the time to call. He went to South America on business and sent me an instant message. He told me how I should have called him. His feelings were hurt. Keep in mind that I have never even met this man.

I thought, "*Maybe the Shrink can help him work things out. Maybe the Needy Photographer can teach the Shrink a thing or two about trust.*"

Enough was enough. I was sure I'd never meet either of them.

The Bartender Comes Again

The Bartender called me regularly. Clearly, we weren't done with each other. He came to see me again. Before he was all the way across my threshold, he was grabbing and kissing me. Knowing what was to come, we quickly grabbed water from the kitchen for the hydration we know we'd need. Then we sprinted to the bedroom. The sex was amazing. Our bodies craved each other. We would kiss, lick and have sex for hours without growing tired. There were no inhibitions. He liked directing me and doing what I was told always brought me to orgasm. Between bouts, we cuddled and talked about life. The time spent together was very sweet. I was myself in his arms. I wasn't an older woman or a cyber date. I wasn't adding mortar to the walls I typically built around myself. I was just me when I was with him. Hours passed. We were always surprised that it was already time for him to leave for work.

The thing about having an affair with a grown man is that you hope he has felt as much sorrow as you have, making the potential for joy that much greater. You hope you will have an overwhelming connection. You hope that your heart and your mind begin to open up to the possibility of what could be.

Hope.

Perhaps this is being ready for the next step. I thought I was ready, but this was clearly not the right man. I was the other woman. In anyone's book, that isn't the proper beginning for the promise of great future potential.

He was feeling remorseful because he discovered he cared about me more than he thought he would. I was remorseful because I should have known better. But still, the attraction to each other was overwhelming.

Truth be told, was falling in love with him. I wanted to share things other than my bed and bedtime stories. I wanted to share other things I loved like the theater and dinosaur bones. We should have agreed to stop seeing each other. If he were a single man, I would have been there in a heartbeat for him.

Now I had something new to cry about.

The Frenchman

While I was waiting for the day to arrive for my final date with The Bartender I realized I must find another distraction or two to try to keep my heart from breaking. I returned to my computer, my old friend, my rock, my long-term relationship. I searched for new emails. Happily, several were waiting. I responded, but my heart wasn't in it. I supposed it was like anything else. Be careful what you wish for. Suddenly, suitors of all ages and shapes buried me. Perhaps I could let go of The Bartender. Maybe my heart wasn't as tied into him as I thought it was.

I was no longer feeling nervous about responding to my suitors, and I was feeling cavalier about who made the cut for this round of dating. I seemed to have crossed some magic line. I was hoping that the line lifted from non-cyber-related suitors as well. Perhaps the cosmos were opening up to the idea of me actually having a man in my life.

The Bartender continued to call me on a daily basis. We made plans for one final meeting. I was resolute that I wouldn't call him. Surely he would leave me be until it was time to confirm our good-bye date. I was more than distracted so I responded to the Frenchman. His emails were charming, and he was young. After a brief instant messaging exchange, he invited me to meet him for coffee. He said he would see me whenever and wherever it was convenient for me. I agreed to meet him and returned to my favorite coffee shop.

On my way to meet the Frenchman, my phone rang. Without my reading glasses on, I wasn't sure who was calling, so just in case it was a new client dying to spend millions on a new apartment, I answered the phone. It was The Bartender. His timing was impeccable. My mind was clear and focused on meeting someone new, and he called. My heart sank. I called a girlfriend for a little reinforcement as I walked down the street to the coffee shop. His phone call quickened my pace. I made it to the coffee shop in record time. Because I was a little early, I found a lovely table. The waitress, who witnessed the Museum Guy fiasco in this same coffee shop, eyed me curiously and seemed to give me a knowing nod. I smiled. To her surprise, yet another man came in to greet me.

The Frenchman was very ... French. He was charming and, surprisingly, much more attractive than his photo. He told me about his business and family and how the curve of my lashes was like the curve of the tip of a rose petal. The waitress was watching me more closely now.

This thirty-seven-year-old man had the demeanor of a much older man. He was sure of himself, and he seemed wise. He certainly made it clear that he had never found an older woman attractive, but he wanted to be near me. At some point in the conversation, he revealed that his father read coffee grounds and that he himself read palms. It was one of the best excuses for holding hands that I'd ever heard. There was no point in resisting. He took my hand and told me what he saw. He took both hands, looked into my eyes, and told me once again how young and lovely I looked. The handholding felt surprisingly intimate. The Frenchman made me so nervous that I knocked over a glass of water, and the waitress rushed over to rescue me. I told him that I must go back to work. This was, of course, a lie, but I knew this date should end for the moment. I still had The Bartender's last call in my ear. The waitress brought our check and raised an eyebrow to me. As we left the coffee shop, he kissed me. He asked when he could see me again. I told him I was booked for the weekend. He said he wouldn't call on Monday because it was his birthday. But he said he'd call me next week to make plans to get together.

I sent him a thank-you email for the lovely afternoon. He responded and told me how lovely my lips tasted. He wondered what I'd like to do on our next date.

I never called him again.

A Farewell to Arms

The time had come to bid farewell to The Bartender. We had arranged to meet in the evening, and we both knew what was to come. Despite that, our passions ran wild. The first kiss was nearly blinding, and we were off to the races.

The Bartender slammed my body against the front door and kissed me as I tore at his clothes. He grabbed me and pushed his hips into my body and growled. "Take your panties off."

The sound of his rough voice telling me what to do made me melt.

We didn't make it more than five feet before he was inside me, my legs thrown over his shoulders and my head just under the dining room table. He took my hands and lifted me up, leading the way to my bedroom. I couldn't get enough of him. I was a woman possessed, clinging to his body and burying my head in his scent.

We took a brief break for a bit of sustenance and then headed back to the bedroom for more. He tormented and pleased me, his mouth on my nipples, his fingers teasing my clit until I begged for him to be inside of me. When he obliged we'd both cry out in ecstasy with me coming again and again.

"Why have I never been witness to one of your infamous hot flashes?"

"I don't seem to have them when I'm having great sex."

I giggled and then we both laughed as he kissed his way down my body and made me come again with his masterful tongue.

The evening was beyond sad, but I was so happy to be in his arms. He held me and told me how much he cared for me. I told him I cared for him as well. We shared our heartaches and dreams regarding love, life, and family. We revealed many secrets. Despite that, he couldn't see a way to move on, and I couldn't see a way to continue to be the other woman. We both cried.

We showered together. Then he dressed to go home, back to her. Neither of us was quite ready to say good-bye, and we embraced while we swayed to Eva Cassidy singing in the background. He kissed me good-bye and walked sadly down the hallway to the elevator. I closed the door and burst into tears as Eva broke into her rousing rendition of "Ain't No Sunshine."

My girlfriends had left messages during his visit. I returned their calls and lied, telling them I was fine.

I cried for the next two days. The night The Bartender left, I cried myself to sleep. When I woke up the next morning, I cried because I could still smell him on the pillow next to me. I couldn't seem to get dressed, so I thought a bubble bath would make me feel better. The sound of my own sobs surprised me as they echoed against the bathroom tile, the same bathroom where he had lovingly washed my hair as we showered together. My cries came from a place so deep inside that I couldn't even describe it. My sorrow was physical, and it consumed me.

I finally got myself out the door and went to my office. The phone rang. It was The Bartender. He called to see how I was doing. I had asked him not to call. He said he wouldn't call, but there he was on the phone saying he missed me; talking about how his day was going. I barely got through the rest of the day. My tears would spring forth for no reason at all, and I didn't know what to do with them.

I reached out to girlfriends, and I think they felt almost as helpless as I did. Was it possible that it had taken me this long to actually fall in love? I had never told my friends I loved him. I never told him I loved him. I never even told myself I was in love with him. Was I really in love? I hadn't been compelled to say it. Neither had he. But it had been years since I cried over a man. In fact, it had been so long that none of my girlfriends had ever witnessed it. In all the years I have been around to live and love, to the best of my recollection, I have only cried such bitter tears twice before.

The Last Time I Cried Real Tears

When I was in my twenties, I was singing in a rock band in New York City. It was the early 1980s. I stayed out late in my pleather jumpsuit and platinum hair. I learned to smoke and drink scotch while my band was doing lines of coke. I tried to live my life on the edge, but it was never lost that I was actually a good girl from North Dakota. In fact, I was remarkably innocent. I was twenty-five years old and still a virgin.

Despite the blush on my cheeks, I was running around the clubs all over town, singing the blues and about love lost like I really understood what that meant. I did come to understand that there was something special about drummers. The quiet guy who sits at the back of the stage says little, but he has all the control. The music flows through their bodies without any words. Every limb, finger, and grunt accentuates each moment, moving in all different directions but all with the right rhythm.

My Drummer was my age, but I thought he held the world in his hands. I was beautiful and sexy and he assumed I was more experienced than I was. I never corrected him. The flirtation continued for some time.

Then I could bear it no more. He was my first, and I fell deeply in love with him. I was sure I never told him. I somehow thought it wasn't done. It wasn't cool. It wasn't part of my pretend image.

In truth, I didn't know how to say it. In fact, I was afraid of the rejection. I was afraid of having my heart broken, so I pushed him away. Stupidly, I couldn't have been more surprised when he actually went with someone else. I didn't think it was real until he moved in with her. He came to see me before he did it, and I pretended like it didn't matter. I somehow thought it would compromise my independence.

I told him that I would never live with someone.

I would never help support someone.

I would never let someone support me.

Never is a big word.

After the Drummer left, I drank so much scotch that I was numb. My heart was broken. To this day, I think it was in my power to mend my own broken heart. I was just too stupid, prideful, afraid, and damaged to ask him to stay with me. Still, I think of him often, and I wonder.

The First Time I Cried

I fell in love in high school. I suppose we all do. I was sixteen years old. He was my very first date, my first kiss, my first dance, my first true passion. We'd kiss for hours with no expectation that things would go any further. When there were no more words to speak, we'd simply breathe at each other on the phone. Within a month of our first date at the Homecoming dance, we were going steady. By Valentine's Day, he asked me to marry him, and I said yes. I was overwhelmed. Of course, I never told my parents when the transition happened from going steady to planning a wedding.

During this time, my mother and I fought madly. In hindsight, I realize she'd have been going through the beginning of menopause. Not only were her hormones running amok, but she had four daughters to cause her grief. At the time, I thought she hated me. Now I know that she was living in a hormonal hell with no one to talk to.

While I was consumed with my teenage hatred of my mother, I clung desperately to the boy I was going to marry. I was sure I loved him. I told him so. He told me he loved me. I had never said those words before to anyone, with the exception of my grandfather who told me he loved me during one of our family visits. I don't remember anyone else ever saying those words to me. I love you.

By the time I was ready to start my senior year in high school, I was sure I had made a mistake. I needed to not be living in a small town and married with children. I wanted to travel and see big cities. I wanted to go to college. I couldn't go through with it. I told him I wouldn't marry him.

On the anniversary of our first date, I went to the Homecoming dance with someone else. As my date walked me to the door and kissed me goodnight, I heard a rustle of footsteps in the leaves. That night, the only boy I ever said I loved drove to the spot where we once parked and kissed for hours. Then he shot and killed himself.

Three Little Words

I love you. The words are so simple, and yet these three syllables bring great joy and nearly break my heart every time I hear them uttered. For some reason, my family started saying them on occasion after my father died. My friends tell me they love me, and now their children do the same. It brings me great joy. I cry at the pure emotion surging through my body like an electric current whenever I think about anyone telling me that he or she loves me. I am learning to say it with ease to my friends, the people I love.

I have still never told a man I love him. I am afraid. I'm afraid of what will happen when I say those three little words. I need someone who is not afraid of the power of my emotions. I guess that's what I'm looking for – someone who won't run from the floodgates that I fear will open when I do say those three little words.

Old Man Brows and Other Hair Sorrows

I have had enough of being maudlin. I needed a distraction, and I was happy to make plans for a date with a Film Maker. As I prepared for my date, I struggled with how to put on mascara while wearing reading glasses. As I peered in the mirror, there it was, a stray, old man hair sprouting from my brow. It was one of those long, wiry hairs you see growing from old men's brows. They tangle together and form a shelf, protecting their faces from the rain.

Nothing could tame it. I tried water. I tried brushing it. I tried styling gel. As a last resort, I tried trimming it. Nothing worked. It stuck straight out, and it was now nearly lethal in its shortened state. I could actually put out someone's eye with it! I decided that, despite the fact I could leave a bald spot in the middle of my brow, I should remove it. I filled in the bald spot with pencil and still met the Film Maker for a smart cocktail. He might have been charming, but it didn't matter. I was sure he was staring at the bald spot in my brow. I drank a martini and politely said goodnight.

A few days later, the temperature dropped a bit. I decided to sport a black turtleneck. I looked in the mirror and to my shock and horror, even without my reading glasses, I could see my sprouting beard against the black background. I shrieked and ran for a pair of reading glasses. It was unbelievable. I tried plucking, but the forest that seemed to be growing from my chin overwhelmed me. I was ashamed. I cursed the hormones surging through my body. Did the onset of menopause mean a lifetime of chin waxing? I couldn't even look at my upper lip! I feared that a handlebar might have grown in the middle of the night. The old man brow should have been a clue. I ran to the local spa that the Polish goddess of hair removal owned. She understood, peered through a high-powered magnifying glass, and got down to business. My chin now felt clean. She cleansed my hairy lip and pruned my old man brows.

Would the curse end here? Or was I destined to later sprout hair from my ears and nose? That idea was too horrible to contemplate so I was content knowing that for the moment, my face was now free of unwanted hair. Once again, I was feminine and ready to date. The Polish goddess did point out that it was time for a facial. She knew I had been dating much younger men. I made an appointment to see her, knowing that, when she was done, my face would be as soft as a baby's bottom.

Unfinished Business

The Bartender provided enough distraction to interrupt at least two rounds of dating. It was no one's fault but my own. I should have powered though and not permitted my infatuation with a man, who I must admit I knew was unavailable, to interrupt my musings.

I thought I'd just start fresh with a new round. I could see if I could impress upon my friends to help find men who did not reside in cyberspace.

In realizing the flaws in my unfinished business with rounds past, I discovered during my quest for a relationship that I was also flawed. I knew I had made bad choices, and I had been unlucky in love. I was also more than lucky. People who would love me forever surrounded me. These people recognized my flaws, even though I was unable to admit that they existed. I realized that it wasn't the same as having a life partner, but the value of the love of friends couldn't be dismissed. They helped to teach me to believe that it was possible to love and trust someone else as much as they loved and trusted me. I had more tears of joy for the love I already had in my life than the tears I had for the loss of The Bartender's love. The best treatment for a broken heart is to embrace the love you receive from the people who you know will love you forever.

Over the next two weeks, The Bartender continued to call me on a daily basis. I was more than happy to hear from him, but it was keeping me from moving on. I told him that it was just too difficult and he had to stop. I said I couldn't talk to him any longer. Days passed, and he didn't call. It took every fiber of my being not to call him. I knew that Valentine's Day was approaching. If he called, I'd be distraught. If he didn't call, I'd be more distraught.

The day arrived, and I knew I had to keep myself busy. Before I was even dressed, I had begun to work. I was so focused that, when the phone rang, I answered it without even looking to see who was calling. It was The Bartender. I was happy and sad at the same time. He called me his "Valentine" and asked if he could bring me flowers. I mustered all of my strength. I intended to tell him that I was happy he called, but the answer was no. I was sure that the word "no" was forming on my lips. But yes came out of my mouth.

I rushed to bathe and dress. He arrived in record time with a dozen apricot, long-stemmed roses. Resistance was futile.

He kissed me, and I crumbled. I cried as we made love. As we languished in each other's arms, I told him in no uncertain terms that he could not see me again unless he was single. I knew he wasn't ready to make that decision, but I knew that I had to draw the line. I deserved better.

As he dressed to go, he said, "I'll call you."

"No."

"Will you call me?" he asked.

"No."

"Can I write to you?" Then, seeing the look on my face, he took it back.

"If you find yourself single, you can call me."

He sat down beside me and said nothing. I told him that he didn't know what he'd be missing. I thought he knew. This time, I thought he might be sadder than I was.

I thought of him daily. I looked up his number on my cell phone again and again, but I resisted hitting Send.

Moving On

I was sure that I had no more tears to shed. It was time to move on. I logged on to the Internet and began to peruse the Web sites once again.

One day, while I was recovering from the man brow incident, I received an email from yet another dating service. I was more than curious. There are dating services for everyone. I can't believe there are so many. This one catered to senior citizens. I decided it was a sign. Perhaps I should be dating someone with giant, wiry brows to rival my own. I logged on and signed up. It couldn't possibly be crazier than any other site I had visited. I wondered if it would be filled with senior citizens and if I would I be the youngster online this time.

I nervously awaited email from AARP members. Then, there it was. I took a deep yoga breath and opened my eyes. The first communication I received was from a forty-four-year-old man. Unbelievable. I never expected that my elderly suitor would be younger than I was.

The Senior Man was thoughtful and sent a lovely email to introduce himself. We exchanged several emails and agreed to meet. He was in the middle of working on a deal, so our date had to wait. He made a reservation for dinner and sent me his photo. We agreed to meet in two weeks for dinner.

Naughty Boy

While I was exchanging email with my charming and age-appropriate Senior Man, another man reached out across cyber space. Yet another young man in search of his Mrs. Robinson. This felt like an epidemic! How could so many young men have the same fantasy? I discussed this issue at length with my girlfriends. We were amazed. How could our bodies, ravaged by gravity and sprouting unwanted hair, be the source of a young man's fantasy? We were surprised, but decided that it was best not to question something so lovely.

This young and Naughty Boy didn't send an email. He started with an instant message.

"Hey baby."

Still experiencing difficulty with multitasking, I actually missed the first one and sent him a thank-you note. Imagine, I thought a young man attempting to send an instant message to a strange, older woman in the middle of the night expected a thank-you note. I sometimes amuse myself and laughed out loud.

The following night, the moment I logged on, he sent me another instant message. The Naughty Boy started by discussing my beauty and moved quickly to telling me how sexy I was. Not surprisingly, I was more than flattered. The discussion went a bit beyond flirtation, but, since I was still aching for The Bartender, I didn't object.

The next evening, it was as if he had been waiting for me to log on. The moment I did, he sent yet another instant message.

"Hey baby."

"Hello."

"I've been thinking about you all day and can't wait to have my way with you."

"What would you like to do to me?"

I couldn't believe I asked.

"I want to run my tongue down your belly and let it linger and play between your legs until you buck and cry out for more."

I couldn't believe how much I liked it.

"You beg me to fill you up in every way. You make me so hard, baby."

I couldn't believe what I was saying back.

"I want to take you in my mouth. Do you feel my tongue licking you and my hair brushing the inside of your thighs?"

We told each other exactly what we would do to each other. We said exactly where our hands and tongues would be. We described how we tasted and how it felt to orgasm.

I didn't think I was ready to meet this man in person, but cybersex was certainly an interesting safe sex alternative. He was more than eager to meet me for coffee. I thought not.

Uncle Fester

While I was trying to forget The Bartender by having cybersex with this young man, I received a charming email from someone new. This new man regaled me with terrible blind date stories that had me in fits of laughter. He had just signed up, so he hadn't put a photo online. Despite that, his humor completely won me over. He admitted to looking like Uncle Fester on the *Addams Family*. Undeterred, I decided to meet him at my favorite coffee shop. Surely the waitress there had missed me. I was also quite sure that this particular meeting would amuse both of us.

I arrived at the coffee shop a little early to settle in and prepare myself for the possibility of having coffee with Uncle Fester. I began to feel a little apprehensive about the fact that there was no liquor available at this establishment. I didn't actually notice when Uncle Fester first entered. What I did notice was the surprised look on the waitress' face. It wasn't a look of concern really; it was one of wonderment and pity. I looked up, and there he was. His bald head floated above a completely black ensemble. He wasn't kidding. I was having coffee with Uncle Fester.

Much to the surprise of both the waitress and me, I had a great time. He was incredibly funny, smart, and charming. Within minutes of the end of our coffee date, he had left me a voice mail. He was charmed and wanted to see me again. I got home, and he had left a lovely email, once more expressing how much he'd like to see me again. I confess that I wasn't attracted to him, but he kept me laughing with his witticisms. He was so smart that I decided I should give this one another try. I agreed to meet him for a movie.

The movie was fun, but I was a bit concerned that he had a flask of scotch in his bag. Uncle Fester explained that he had had a very bad day but, even in my misspent youth, I never sucked scotch from a sack during a movie.

Despite the fact he had a couple of belts during the movie, I agreed to join him for a drink afterwards. Again, his smart conversation charmed me, but it wasn't enough to be more than his friend. I went home a bit too tipsy. By the time I got there, he had left me two messages and an email discussing my many charms.

While it was true I had won the affections of Uncle Fester, I couldn't reciprocate. I enjoyed his company, but it would be wrong to encourage him. He continued to send email. I just stopped responding.

My Body Is On Fire

The hot flashes continued. The waves of heat rippling through my body only served as a reminder that my body and soul ached for a man. I seemed to have a need for male contact, a need for sex that was more than just a passing fancy. Do other menopausal women experience this same blind lust? My libido seemed to be epic in size. I constantly contemplated the male form.

I missed The Bartender, but knew I shouldn't even consider him as an option for my relief. I briefly considered the idea of sex for the sake of sex, but I realized I wasn't cut out for it. I didn't want to put my fire out. I wanted to find someone who could keep it burning. I wanted someone who would fan the flames so they'd never go out. I couldn't explain exactly what I was looking for, but I felt sure I'd recognize him, the man who welcomed my tears and breathed in life from my laughter. At the same time, I feared that person didn't exist and that I'd been alone for so long that my fantasy was just that. I cried and refused to believe that was true. I had to believe the man for me was out there. If not, I'd be unable to go on. I had to believe it.

I had to have hope. Once again, the tears began to flow.

I cried because I was happy that I still felt hopeful.

Unwanted Attentions

I seemed to be emitting pheromones that alerted men of all ages to my situation. I had no control over my body. Walking down the street, men turned their heads and smiled. I went to a diner slovenly dressed and without any makeup on, yet men glanced in my direction and winked while waiting for my response. Could they really know how I felt? Were they merely responding to the residual heat emitting from my body because of the rapid succession of hot flashes?

I was, as they say, in a pickle. I didn't want to call The Bartender. The thought of Uncle Fester was just too much to think about. I focused on my pending date with the Senior Man. His photo was quite handsome, and I was hopeful for some kind of relief.

Senior Man arranged for us to meet at a lovely midtown Manhattan restaurant that I'd been dying to try. I spent quite a bit of time deciding what to wear. While showing up naked would make my intent for the evening clear, it was perhaps a bit too direct. I decided to wear a skirt even though I seldom show my legs. It was incredibly cold outside, but I was donning a suede skirt with a silk blouse and very high heels with toe cleavage. My hair and makeup looked great.

I arrived, and he was waiting at the bar. I pretended not to notice as he looked up from his smart cocktail and drank me in. He was clearly pleased. He had a few more pounds than I expected, but he was handsome and charming with an English accent. We chatted over drinks and then went up to the dining room for a scrumptious dinner. Our conversation flowed easily. We discussed the theater, the state of real estate, and the silliness of dating in middle age.

Senior Man lived just a few blocks away from the restaurant. Had he selected this particular dinner spot with something more in mind? Could he sense the fire burning within me? I took his arm as we walked up the avenue in the bitter cold. He sweetly kissed me goodnight and put me in a cab. I was disappointed and assumed I would never hear from him again.

I was busy the next day at work. I was running around town all day, showing apartments to customers. I was more than surprised when my phone rang and Senior Man was on the other end, asking when I might be available to see a movie. You could have knocked me over with a feather. I agreed to meet him the following evening.

For our second date I decide a more casual approach was in order. I wore jeans and a loose sweater. Thank goodness I had on a T-shirt under my sweater. Before the lights dimmed for previews, I was having my first hot flash. I tried not to look too desperate as I ripped the sweater over my head. He tried not to notice, but I was sure he could feel the heat radiating from my body. I was like a furnace. As the sweat on my brow turned to steam, my hair curled and frizzed out from my head. Halfway through the film, I was so cold that I had to put my clothes back on.

Once the movie was over, despite my wild mane, he asked if I'd like to have a bite to eat. It was much later than I liked to dine, but I willingly agreed and decided to take this handsome man to one of my favorite haunts. It was a fabulous bistro, and yes, The Bartender's bar. I realized The Bartender wasn't scheduled to work that evening, but I knew I might be stirring things up. We were seated at a lovely table, and the usually friendly staff ignored me. I was clearly on a date. I always wondered if they knew about The Bartender and me?

I turned my complete attention to Senior Man. He seemed very comfortable with me. Then it happened. There is something about me that causes people to share their darkest feelings. People I barely know feel comfortable sharing things that are typically reserved for their therapists.

And so it began. He shared the reasons for the demise of his marriage. It was still clearly very new. He still referred to her as "my wife."

Finally I had to ask, "Are you still married?"

He said, "Yes."

His marriage was clearly over. Just the same, he was heartbroken, and it would take years for this tragic story to be over. I wasn't sure who was more stunned. For me, I couldn't believe what I was hearing. For him, he couldn't believe what he was sharing. It couldn't possibly have been his intent to share his story of loss and betrayal with me that evening. He might as well have told me then and there that he wouldn't be calling. He had shared too soon. We left the restaurant. He gave me a quick kiss goodnight in the cold and put me in a cab.

His last words to me were, "I'll call you."

There are no more final words said during the beginning of a doomed relationship.

I left him a message, thanking him for the evening and never heard from him again. So much for the relief of my burning body, and just like in life, I realized that there is sometimes no lesson to be learned.

A Shift in Focus

It was remarkably busy at work. While you may or may not think so, real estate is a seasonal business. Spring was approaching, and everyone would feel like making a change. It was time to make the big push, nab those new apartments to sell, and coddle buyers so they'd remember that I was their gal when it was time to buy. I was working weekends and preparing for an out-of-town sales convention. I tried to forget the fire burning within my body, but it couldn't be done.

I found myself killing time at a quiet open house by reading a book that The Bartender recommended. He still called me regularly. I tried to resist, but it was hard with the constant reminders he delivered. On the eve of my business trip, I couldn't resist any more. I agreed to let him come over one last time. Undeterred, I pressed him to explain himself.

"What do you want?" he asked.

"Why won't you leave me be?"

He shrugged.

"Are you really surprised by my growing feelings in response to your attentions?"

He had nothing to say. He was suddenly reserved.

He was unable to express any feelings or emotions. He told me that he was feeling too vulnerable to talk about it, but he couldn't resist seeing me. I told him that I'd ask again for a more honest answer and that he needed to give it some serious thought.

I left town for a week and successfully resisted making any calls. I conducted some serious networking business, and I was the life of the office parties. Of course, I found a bit of time to ensure I had a tan line by the time I got home.

Upon my return, I looked fantastic. I agreed to meet a friend for a smart cocktail so The Bartender could get a good look at what he was missing. He greeted me with a kiss. He touched my face from the other side of the bar. He held my hands and talked softly. This couldn't possibly be the conduct of a man having a secret affair. I was inspired to leave a naughty message on his cell phone while I was still sitting at the bar, but I immediately wished I could take it back. He called me a couple of days later with nothing to say. He called again and still offered nothing. I felt foolish for wanting to hear more. While I, of course, would prefer to hear what I wanted, I'd be happy with an honest discussion. He had lost his ability to converse. My need for openness has somehow silenced him. I was angry and once again I resolved that enough was enough. Only time would tell if I could remain strong, but I was ready to move on. There were many apartments to be sold and even more men to be dated. That being said, what I really wanted to know was if my judgment about this man had been true or if he had made a fool of me.

Sharing

I wasn't sure what I should be doing at this point. My base desires were still getting the best of me. Incredibly, I longed for romance as I muddled through my endless days of work. Hormones were rocking my world. I still cried at least once a day. I sometimes cried for myself and I sometimes cried for someone else, but I always cried.

The other day, the sky turned periwinkle with streaks of pink as the sun was setting. I had to stop walking down the sidewalk to cry at the sheer beauty of the colors. I was finding it easier to share how I was feeling about what was happening in my life. I discovered that it was okay to cry as I shared my feelings with my friends, and they were feeling better about letting me do it. I was constantly surprised by others' reactions to the changes in me. For the most part, the reaction had been positive. A few were frightened by what I viewed as progress in my personal journey. They seemed shocked and uneasy with the idea of my being candid about my life with them.

One day, in an effort to show how comfortable he

was with my sharing, a friend actually suggested I must be relieved to know I could feel things deeply. While I was sure the comment wasn't intended to harm, I was cut to the quick. Apparently, he never considered that I did have feelings all along, but I had never actually shared them with him. Did others find me to be a rock with no cracks at all?

The thought of that conversation still makes me weep. The tears don't come from a place of hurt as much as they come from a place of loss. If this was indeed how others viewed me, how many times had I shut a door without actually knowing it was open? Had I missed my chance for happiness simply because I was too quick to close the door?

At the same time, one of my best friends let me know that she could tell by the tone of my voice when I have spoken to The Bartender or when I had a good or bad day. She heard the emotion in my voice. I'd typically shut down, refusing to expose my soft underbelly any further. Happily, her insight relieved me. I cried because I thought she might love me forever as I loved her.

Round Nine

So now it was time for the ninth round of dating. Compared to other rounds, more men were rejected in this one, but I was trawling around the Internet, searching for the perfect man.

One evening, as I wandered through cyberspace on my continued quest to stop my hot flashes, I thought I might have found my man. His profile was perfect. He mentioned one of my favorite spots. He was age-appropriate. Even though he was so new on the site and still didn't have a photo posted, I sent an email. He quickly responded with an invitation for coffee. I agreed to meet him and asked what he looked like. He told me that he looks like a young Johnny Carson. I agreed to meet him at my favorite coffee shop. I arrived, and the regular waitress looked suspicious.

I was on time. Spotting no one who looked like Johnny, I sat at an empty table. The waitress looked at me as if I were doing something wrong. As I opened my paper to read, a gentleman came from the men's room. Here's Johnny!

He did look like Johnny Carson. Actually, he

looked more like Johnny's poor relation. He sat down and starting dropping the names of celebrities he was working with on his various film projects. I couldn't have been less impressed or more bored. Even the waitress looked bored. Finally, my coffee cup was empty, and it was over.

The Cyber Date

After Johnny, so many emails came in from the various sites I had joined that it was overwhelming. With each block, I was sent another hit. One communication was surprising, and I was so lonely that I responded. He was beautiful. Studly Nightshade was a stunning specimen of a man who sent a charming and smart email. I agreed to call him, and he immediately made it clear that he was interested in two things: a big butt and sex with the person who had that big butt. He was going to miss on both counts. So much for him. Someone that beautiful was clearly too good to be true.

All was not lost. That very evening, while recovering from a particularly bad day of hot flashes, I received an instant message from a gentleman who said he had recently relocated from the West Coast to expand his business. He also didn't have a photo posted, but his messages were kind, respectful, and fun. He asked me to go out for dinner with him at that very moment.

Relocation Man began our cyber date by picking me up in his car. We discussed our wardrobe and the drive down the highway to one of his favorite restaurants. He had even called ahead to arrange for a dessert soufflé to follow the sumptuous dinner he had ordered. My hormones were running amok. All day long, one hot flash after another had consumed me. Now Relocation Man's words were soothing me as they appeared on my computer screen.

His description of the sunset was so beautiful that I actually cried even though we weren't in the same location. It was one of the most romantic dates I ever had.

The next morning, he called. We easily chatted for an hour before I had to leave for work. We made plans to meet, and he called daily as the actual date drew nearer. On the day of the date, I was excited. I confess I even put on a scarf that was reminiscent of what I had worn on our cyber date.

I arrived at the coffee shop a bit early, settled in with my paper, and ordered a cappuccino. Time passed. I finished most of the *New York Times*. My regular waitress was looking worried; I was looking foolish. I had never waited more than thirty minutes for anyone. Not ever. Despite that, there I sat, pretending to be fascinated with my newspaper. I have no idea what I read. An hour went by. I calmly paid my bill and left the coffee shop.

An hour later, I received a call from Relocation Man, apologizing for the change of plans. I was outraged that he hadn't called me earlier in the day. He said he had. He was beside himself and I was fool enough to believe him. He claimed that a work-related emergency had kept him away. I could hear stress in his voice. After several calls, I decided to forgive him.

Later that night, we had another cyber date. This one was more intimate.

"I'd love to take you dancing," he said. "I know a little supper club where they have live big band music."

"I'd love that!" I was already swooning.

"I'm driving down the highway on my way to see you wearing a deep blue suit. I have a gift for you."

"I can't wait for you to get here."

"What are you wearing?"

"A black cocktail dress. Low cut, showing off a bit of cleavage. Very fitted at the waist but the skirt is full and falls just above my knee. I'm wearing black patent heels."

"And…"

"And?"

"What are you wearing under that dress?"

I knew what he wanted to hear. "Stockings. Very sheer. Black. Just up to my thighs. The garter belt is also black and very lacy, but the straps running down my thighs from the belt to the stockings are a lovely emerald green."

"I arrive at your door and you let me in."

"You look very handsome in your blue suit."

"I move to you and softly kiss those red lips."

"Is that a present in your pocket or are you happy to see me?"

"You are a funny woman," he teased. "You need to do something for me first before I give you your present."

"Anything," I replied waiting for his request to appear on my screen.

"I want to see a bit of the green of your garter

belt."

"I slowly raise my skirt and watch your eyes travel from my heels, up my leg to the top of my stocking so that you can see just a bit of skin and you smile. I raise my skirt just a bit higher so you can take a peek at the green of my garter belt tugging at my stocking."

"Don't move. I'm walking slowly over to you so I can touch that bit of skin between your stocking and your skirt. My finger traces the edge of your stocking."

"I gasp at your touch."

"I put my arms around your waist and pull you in to kiss you."

"My body falls into your arms and I feel myself surrender."

"I can feel it. I kiss your cleavage then run my fingers along the edge of your dress along your breasts."

"My breath quickens."

"I pull you in to kiss you hard and unzip your dress."

"My dress falls to the floor."

"Lovely."

"I was feeling a bit naughty as I dressed and thought of you, so I am not wearing panties."

"I can see that."

"I'm getting wet in anticipation of your touch."

"I reach down and touch your pubic hair. Teasing. My hand reaches between your slightly open legs but only teasing, barely touching."

"I gasp at your touch."

"I reach into my pocket and take out a red box for you to open."

"Cartier?"

"Of course. A lovely emerald necklace to match your garter belt. It falls just so the end touches the peak of your cleavage and I kiss your breasts on either side."

"It's perfect. Thank you."

"Don't move. I want to look at you."

"Whatever you say."

"I walk around you as I take off my clothes, admiring your legs, your ass, your breasts rising and falling."

"I can see your lovely erection as you come around to admire the front of my body."

"Yes. I am so hard right now."

"And I am so wet."

"How are you going to thank me for that necklace, baby?"

"I step closer to you and kiss you. In a moment I am on my knees, my red lips wrapping around your delicious cock."

"I love watching your mouth on my cock."

"My hands move around to squeeze your ass while my mouth takes you in."

"I see you move a hand to touch yourself as you suck on my hard cock."

"Yes. I am feeling so sexy kneeling before you in my garter belt and bra."

"I love that you want to please me."

"I do."

"I pull your hair again and tilt your head so I can see your face. I kneel down so I can kiss you and touch that wet pussy myself."

"I gasp at your touch and beg you to be inside of

me."

"Are you touching yourself for me?"

"Yes."

"Good girl. I'd love to fuck you so hard."

"Yes."

"I thrust inside of you until you scream for me to come."

"I'm ready. I want to hear you come."

My phone rang and I listened as he came. I loved that even from so far away I could make him come on command.

He called often. I was developing quite a crush. We planned to meet again. This time, when it was time to confirm, he just disappeared. I was more than angry. He was like the Chef, hiding somewhere, locked in a room never to come out. He called and explained his grandmother had died. I felt bad for thinking ill of him. He was going to stay with his family for a while.

I don't know why, but he was getting under my skin. I found him intriguing, but he was yet another man who revealed nothing really tangible about himself. I had no photo, phone number, or address. I did have his actual email address. I was beginning to feel foolish. How much of what he said was real? We'd occasionally have online conversations. He'd occasionally call me on the phone, but it always from an unlisted number. Again, I was feeling suspicious. Was I being lied to? Could men in prison send email? Was he under house arrest?

Even though we never met, I strangely seemed to be developing feelings for him. Relocation Man had become an emotional replacement for The Bartender. I was being silly and vulnerable. I was becoming the definition of desperate. I felt so sad that I cried myself to sleep.

The First Brick

My friends are telling me that I'm being too sensitive. I cry at the drop of a hat. It might be my fluctuating hormones, but the fact of the matter is I've always been a big crier. I still cry at the drop of a hat, but I have begun to welcome the openness, the honesty with which I am beginning to treat my own feelings. I surprise myself at my willingness to at least try to be vulnerable. It's an amazing sensation after having spent nearly a half-century on guard.

My father was in the military during my formative years. Each time we moved, I would become what I thought was expected in each new school. I'd be dramatic. I'd be fun. I'd be exotic, eating only mustard on my hamburgers. I'd cry in the lunchroom over the death of a much-loved pet that never existed. The effect was quite compelling. My newfound friends surrounded the exciting newcomer.

My parents never knew of my secret life. I'm sure they were in their own adjustment period each time we moved. They'd go out a lot, probably to make new friends, leaving my older sister and me to fend for ourselves. A few years later, we became surrogate mothers to our new baby sisters. I struggled to find my way, to discover who I was and to understand what and how I felt.

One of the most defining moments in my life happened when I was around ten years old. I confess I don't recall the incident that was the catalyst, but, as my punishment was being doled out, my mother asked if I felt angry. I was paralyzed. I didn't know what to say. I was suddenly terrified. What was the right answer? If I said yes, would that be sassing back? Would I receive a harsher punishment? If I said no, would the result be the same?

I stood there, weak-kneed with my heart pounding and tears welling up in my eyes. Finally, the only words I thought were safe to utter came out of my mouth.

"I don't know."

"You're not allowed to be angry."

My mother's response would shape my emotional growth. At that moment, the first bricks and mortar were laid at my feet. It was the foundation for the walls to come. I have often replayed that moment. It has been my tool for coping with emotion, my attempt to stay on an even keel with the world, to hold on to the expectation that I could control any situation without feeling.

Now as my hormones have taken hold, I have come to realize what a foolish expectation that is. How much have I missed because I refused to let others know I was hurt or happy? I am horrified and freed at the same time. Each day, there is something to be happy about, to cry about, or both. I am trying to share those moments not only with others but with myself as well. I am learning that it is okay to let others in on my big secret.

I cry.

I bleed.

I succeed.

I fail.

I am happy.

I am lonely.

I am scared.

I am fearless.

I am freer than I have ever been.

I am feeling cavalier about breaking down my walls. The loss of boundaries is making me cautious and reckless at the same time. I worry about myself and try to remember to tell my friends what adventures I am up to. I don't believe I have put myself in danger as I attempt to date the entire Eastern seaboard, but I do realize that perhaps I am not the best judge of my situation since I am allowing myself to feel in front of others for the first time.

The Italian Knight

I am feeling beyond sad since The Bartender stepped out of my life. I cry every day and can think of nothing but sex. I am feeling unloved and unlovable. I am feeling reckless. I'm not sure if what I want is to try and hurt The Bartender by having sex with someone else or if I've given up and am in search of all I have always believed I deserve, to face up to the reality that I could never truly being loved by a man. I wanted to have anonymous sex with a stranger and not care. I wanted to take out my anger and the wrath of my broken heart on a man who wanted nothing more than to fuck me.

Late one night I was surfing through cyberspace with way too much scotch in my system and I decided to post an erotic profile on a website that clearly existed for the sole purpose of hooking up. My profile consisted of 2 badly crafted sentences and no photograph.

Beautiful redhead with large breasts. Can think of nothing but sex.

Within seconds of the post going live I was bombarded with requests. It wasn't surprising that most of the responses were vulgar. After all, it was a sex site. My in box was filled with misspelled missives and pictures of penises from various angles, but all up close. I somehow hoped that there would be a man out there who would sense my broken heart and want to make sure I was alright, but all I got was a mailbox full of men who thought their penises were so unique and so lovely that I required a penis portrait.

I spent a couple of nights thinking about what might happen if an email with complete sentences came my way. I barely had time to register that thought, when a lovely, lengthy spell-checked email arrived. Forgetting I was in a forbidden zone of cyberspace, I happily responded to the Italian Knight. He was a true New Yorker of Italian decent and, based on his turn of a phrase, well educated. The Italian Knight shared stories of his divorce, children and business and, though I had not seen his picture, I went with my gut instinct and agreed to meet him for a drink.

It was a bit nippy outside so I wore my black wool coat over a pair of black trousers and a low-cut frilly black blouse that allowed my breasts to peek out. My makeup looked good and I was having an amazingly good hair day. I was eager to meet my Italian Knight. I somehow imagined that he would ride up on his white horse and save me from my dilemma. It wasn't until I found myself sitting at a neighborhood bar ordering a smart cocktail that I remembered I was meeting a man that I had just met on an Internet sex site.

My heart began to race as I sipped at my glass of scotch to calm my nerves. I considered running out the door, but just as I reached to grab my coat, a very handsome, very normal looking man walked in the door and smiled at me. His hair was brown and full with just a little bit of gray at the temples. His eyes seemed kind, although I couldn't tell the color in the dimly lit bar. When he smiled at me I swore his teeth sparkled as if he had popped out of a cartoon.

"Michelle?"

This handsome man with the sparkly teeth was my date. I was relieved and stunned speechless. All I could do was nod my head in response.

"What a relief," he said as he shed his coat and took a seat beside me at the bar. "I was so nervous. I had no idea what I as in for."

"You?!" I laughed. "I was just getting ready to run out the door. I began to convince myself that a two-headed killer in a clown suit was coming to meet me."

"What are you drinking?" he asked.

"Scotch."

"I'll have what she's having." He said to the bartender. The Italian Knight added a couple of appetizers to the order and then looked at me curiously.

"You're blushing."

I nodded.

"You are full of surprises aren't you? What made a woman who still blushes sign up for that website?"

"I was lonely and feeling a bit wild, I guess."

"Well lucky me."

"How about you?" I asked.

"I guess I'm a typical man. I was looking for two hot women who might be looking for me." He laughed at the shocked look on my face and dimples appeared on his cheeks. "I was just kidding," he said and smiled again. "That was never going to happen, but I did find you."

I was nervous again. This man was handsome, charming, funny, smart, adorable, and a whole host of other things I couldn't think of at the time. If I had met him on one of the other dating websites I wouldn't have thought twice about letting him seduce me, but this felt tawdry. He touched my hand and told me how lovely I looked. He assured me that if I was too nervous he completely understood, but that he found me very attractive. I delayed and giggled and gushed over how delicious the appetizers were. I watched him as he ran his finger down my forearm and over my hand. Then he looked into my eyes, smiled and kissed me. It was a soft and gentle kiss and I loved every second of it.

"I understand if you don't want to" he said, "but I'd love to see you naked."

I wanted to be ravaged by this man and at the same time didn't want him to think I was a 'bad girl.' I honestly don't know what that was all about. Being 'bad' was the whole idea, the whole reason we were meeting. I was torn. How ridiculous that the only thing in my head that was making me think about saying no was that it felt too dirty. I gulped back my drink and agreed to let him walk me home. I felt him breathe in my scent as he helped me on with my coat.

As soon as we arrived at my door I invited him up for a nightcap. I took his coat and was happy to see he was even more handsome in the light of my apartment. As I began to pour us both a drink, he took the glasses out of my hands and kissed me. Hungrily I kissed him back.

He smiled. "You're full of surprises, aren't you?"

My eyes glanced down as I felt my cheeks go red again. The Italian Knight brushed my hair off my neck and kissed it as he began to unbutton my blouse. He leaned in to kiss my breasts, following the line of my bra with each kiss. I reached up to stop his progress.

"Do you want me to go?"

"No."

"Do you want me to stop?"

"No."

"Do you want to take me to bed?"

I took his hand and led him down the yellow hallway to my bedroom. Perhaps it was the scotch, or the reason that brought us together, but I don't remember a lot about that first night. I do remember letting him kiss every inch of my body as he undressed me, and how his slow progress made me ache to have him inside of me. I don't remember him removing his own clothing, but I do remember him slowly pushing me back onto my bed and feeling his warm skin against mine, the weight of his body on mine, asking where my condoms were, and then a blurry dance of sin and sex and sweat until we were nothing but a quivering mass, exhausted from the orgasms and sheer exercise of it all. He spooned me and pulled the duvet up to cover us and I fell asleep in his arms.

I do remember the next morning. I remember waking to his dimples and seeing that his eyes were brown. I remember how it felt to have his fingers trace up my leg to my waist and then feeling his warm mouth on my breasts and the smell of his hair making me wet. I remember how it felt to wrap my legs around him as he entered me and kissed my neck and how the muscles of his legs felt beneath my touch. I remember how lovely it was to linger in bed and discuss making plans to see each other again.

The Italian Knight and I had several dates. We had both reached out in the middle of the night with broken hearts and stumbled upon each other, but our brief romance ended abruptly.

My Italian Knight fell off his horse when, rather than having the courage to see me one last time, he wrote me a long email explaining that he was still in love with someone else. I cried myself to sleep because I thought he would be the one to chase The Bartender from my dreams. Perhaps if we had met at a different time or under better circumstances we would have been a match, but I think the way we met colored everything. Of course, there was that small detail that I too was still in love with someone else.

Meanness

Weeks had passed since my last encounter with The Bartender, the encounter that was supposed to be our final good-bye. My attempt to fall in love with someone else had failed, but I somehow felt better knowing that I could possibly find love in another man's arms.

Out of the blue The Bartender called.

"How are you beautiful?"

"Why are you calling me?"

"I really don't have the time to talk right now."

"So why did you call?"

"Look, I've got to run, but I've been thinking about you a lot. I care about you and didn't want you to think I'd forgotten about you."

I met his response with silence.

"I told you I'd call."

"Are you single?"

"I really can't talk right now. Can we meet for breakfast?"

"Is this a new ploy for sex?" I wondered.

"No," is all I could say as I tearfully hung up the phone.

I never understood why he called if he didn't have time to talk. Did he call so I could be the one to say he was out of line? So I could be the one to sound needy? So he could have the position of power? So I could be angry?

I was all of those things. I felt needy and powerless and angry. I was still hurting over the end of my brief romance with Italian Knight and The Bartender was calling to remind me how much I missed him. I was aching to be loved and couldn't bear another rejection. I think The Bartender called just to make a power play, just to be mean.

I'll never understand why people find that meanness is the solution for separation? If he truly cared for me, why would he be so selfish and hateful? I can understand the hurtful things said during a fight, the words that escape from deep within and slice like daggers through the air. We never mean to say those words that will be quickly retracted and hopefully forgiven, but when the time has come to stop seeing someone, someone you care for, why not just kiss, say good-bye, and wish happiness for each other? You both know that is what's best. Is the separation somehow made easier by dismissing the other's existence on earth? Do we somehow feel less foolish by making the other person feel angry and foolish rather than admitting the obvious error in judgment?

The Bartender continued his teasing calls and they made me furious. I was resentful, and I felt like saying hateful things. He made me feel small, so I wanted to make him feel the same way. I hated that. I wanted to call him back because I needed to discover if it were true that I had made such an error in judgment.

I am usually a good judge of character and situations. I may not always make the right choice. I knew that going in, but I am seldom wrong about a situation. I couldn't believe I had been so gullible. I felt that everything that had passed between us was a lie.

Other lovers from my past came to my house for dinner with their wives. The Bartender didn't want to honestly state his case. It was easier to make me be the one to be saved, to make me the wounded one. If I allowed myself to be the victim, I would lose a piece of myself. For the moment, I refused.

Spring

The problem with this particular personal transition was that it was springtime and I definitely had spring fever. Spring is also one of the busiest times of the year in New York real estate. My hormones were raging and, once again, my multitasking skills were challenged. I failed miserably.

One Saturday I left my house with the specific intention of running errands and picking up a few sundries at a local drugstore. I was focused and ready for the task at hand. I left my house and walked up the street. On my way, I passed by the manicure shop. I stopped and asked if they could fit me in. I was thrilled that in ten minutes they could see me. Besides, it was time for the removal of my ever-sprouting facial hair. I ran up the street, heading toward the drugstore. On my way, I passed by Starbucks. Even though it was only fifty degrees outside, a hot flash pulled me in to order a large iced beverage.

As I tried to pay for my iced latte, I couldn't seem to figure out what bills to pull from my pocket. My phone rang, and, luckily, I had on reading glasses. I could see that this was a call I should answer. As I flipped open my phone, at least sixty dollars was now on the counter to pay for my latte. The man behind the register looked confused.

I forgot that when one answers the phone it was customary to speak. After moments of silence, I suddenly heard someone shouting out, "Hello!" Surprised, I responded, tried to collect my change, and announced to the entire population of Starbucks that I couldn't be held responsible for my actions. I explained that multitasking was impossible for a perimenopausal woman, especially during a hot flash.

I set off with my iced beverage into the nippy morning and proceeded to get a manicure and have the new crop of hair ripped from my chin. Two hours after I left home, I arrived back in my apartment. Not only did I not do the one thing I had left the house to do, but I had no memory of why I was going to the drugstore in the first place.

I needed to do something constructive. I had dry cleaning to do and planned a visit to a local establishment for a business meeting. I headed back out the door. When I arrived at the dry cleaners, I discovered I had left my house without the clothes. I had gone too far to turn back, so I headed to the restaurant for my business meeting. The man I was to meet wasn't there. The pitiful truth is that I knew he wouldn't be there, but had somehow forgotten that fact. I turned back on my heels. As I headed back home, I passed another drugstore. I entered with purpose and then proceeded to walk up and down each aisle, trying to recall why I was there. Unsuccessful, I walked out the door. As I left the drugstore I spotted the dry cleaners and had to remind myself that I had no laundry with me.

On the way home, I stopped to buy five lemons for one dollar just so I'd have some sense of accomplishment for the day.

Possession

My body was possessed. The hot flashes were constant. The only thing that seemed to be able to cool my face was the constant stream of tears that would spring forth every hour on the hour. I couldn't stop the tears. The sadness within me felt like another person trying to escape. Surely this deep sorrow couldn't be mine. I needed an exorcism. I struggled to find the source of my sorrow.

I was lonely.

I was lonely for a best friend. I wanted someone who would be by my side through thick and thin. I wanted someone who wouldn't be afraid of my tears. I wanted someone who'd want to stay with me even when I tried to push him away.

I was beyond lonely.

My raging hormones barely gave me a break between hot flashes. Even so, I thought the truth was that the loneliness is real. My raging hormones were making me feel so insecure that I couldn't hide the loneliness from myself any longer and the power of my own emotion scared me.

Making matters worse, in addition to the hot

flashes and the tears, I seemed to have an uncontrollable urge for sex. Every second of every hour of every day, I thought of nothing but men. Even my dreams were filled with wild scenes from romance novels. I didn't know if this was a response to the feelings of loneliness or if I truly needed sex. I felt like an exposed nerve. I cried and was filled with elation at the same time. I was so easily aroused that I surprised myself. Even a bumpy cab ride excited me. I felt like one of those pitiful boys in junior high school who got an erection each time a girl walked down the hall. My only saving grace was that no one could see my erection. Just the thought of being close to another man nearly brought me to orgasm. I am sure this mix of emotion and sensation is partially responsible for sending so women in search of anti-anxiety medication during menopause. How else can anyone balance the internal madness brought on by every day life?

The Englishman

I was feeling desperate, both emotionally and sexually. I was crying more regularly and The Bartender was ever present on my mind. I obsessively surfed the Internet in search of a man. I couldn't leave it alone.

On my journey through cyberspace one night, a request for a chat session flashed up on my screen.

"Hello, lovely."

Yet another young man desiring an older woman was on the other end. I took a gander at his profile before responding. This one had a twist. He was in England. If I could believe his profile, he was handsome, smart, and charming with adorable dimples and only thirty-four years old.

"Hello, handsome."

"What's a lovely woman like you doing in a place like this? ;-)"

"LOL! What are you doing chatting up an older woman on the other side of the pond?"

"I love older women."

"Why is that?"

"You know what you need. Fancy a young British

cock?"

I was a bit surprised at the abrupt mention of cock, but excited by it as well. We chatted for some time, but it didn't take long for things to take a very naughty turn. I was surprising myself at the words that were coming from the tips of my fingers and landing onto the screen. It was a lesson learned from my encounters with the Naughty Boy.

"What are you wearing?"

"A lovely black silk robe."

"And?"

"And my nipples are brushing against the silk as my robe falls open."

"I'd like to pinch those nipples for you."

"Suck them."

"Yes, darlin."

"My legs spread wider for you."

"Do you have a webcam?"

"No."

"Do you want to watch me?"

In another first for me this year, I accepted his invitation.

There he was in all his glory, thirty-four years old, six-foot-three, slender, handsome, and naked as the day he was born. Clearly aroused, I egged him on. His pleasure excited me. The only thing he had to guide him was the power of my words.

"Imagine my hand beneath yours, stroking that lovely cock."

I watched his hand in a steady stroke on my computer screen.

"Kneeling between those legs, my tongue flicking the head of your cock."

A smile flashed on his face.

"Running my tongue the length of your cock and then taking your head in my mouth. Sucking."

As I watched him stroke himself and smile I could feel myself getting wet. In his excitement he bumped into the computer and my view was gone.

"Move the camera," I snapped.

Dutifully he moved the camera as I promised to climb on top of his beautiful cock and ride him until he came.

"I need to hear your voice."

I quickly typed my number and then talked to him, listening to his quickening breath as I watched him climax across the ocean.

The next morning, the Englishman sent me emails and further instant messages regarding his life and business in hopes of another cyber date. I hungrily obliged him with more chat and Web cam sessions.

The Scientist

As my transatlantic cyber affair continued and my body ached for The Bartender, an attractive, age-appropriate, geographically desirable man, employed as a scientist arrived on the scene. After the exchange of a couple of funny emails and a quick phone conversation, we agreed to meet at the Museum of Natural History to peruse dinosaur bones.

The date was delightful. We grabbed a bite for lunch, then wound our way through the museum, and headed into Central Park, talking and laughing all the while. It was still very cool out, and we nestled into a park bench for warmth as we shared more of our stories. The date ended with a walk to the subway and a quick kiss good-bye.

As he was presumably globetrotting and buried with work, I'd have occasional emails from him on his travels, suggesting we try to catch up in person soon. My friends were all rooting for this funny and smart man. If the truth be told, so was I. There was no initial spark with The Scientist, but I liked him and thought that, perhaps if the wind whirling around me from The Bartender died down, I could build a fire with The Scientist.

Foot Man

The days were beginning to get warmer, and my hot flashes were hotter. My spring fever was raging, and The Scientist was nowhere to be found and I began to question whether he was married. My only male contact was with the Englishman who kept reappearing on my screen. I needed to get a hold of myself. This was no way for a grown woman to act. I was enjoying the salacious nature of my encounters with the Englishman. It was my dirty little secret. This transatlantic cyber relationship seemed harmless and safe, and I was quite comfortable keeping the naughty details all to myself.

Just as Memorial Day was approaching, I received a charming email from a local suburban man who regaled me with compliments. We spoke on the phone a couple times and despite his overwhelming New Jersey accent and occasional mysterious reference to feet, I agreed to meet him one morning for a walk in the park.

On the day we met, Foot Man arrived in New York two hours early and called to let me know. His eagerness was somehow alarming. I agreed to meet him a bit earlier.

I walked the ten blocks from my apartment to the park and was shocked to be greeted by what must have been my date's evil twin in a shiny tracksuit. This was not the handsome man from the online photos. I couldn't believe we were in my neighborhood and in my park. What if someone I knew saw us together?

His accent echoed throughout the park. I thought that perhaps sitting rather than walking would quiet him down a bit. As we sat, he dropped to the ground in front of me, yanked my shoe off and began to rub my foot. He told me that he wanted to be my foot slave. Despite my advanced years, no one had ever uttered those words in my presence. To my knowledge, none of my friends had ever heard those words in any of their sexcapades either. Amazingly, his shiny tracksuit was armed with foot lotion. Holding on tightly to my foot, he removed his glasses and brushed his nose against my toes. As calmly as I could, I removed my foot from his grip, stood up, and walked out of the park. He followed me as I directed him to the subway. My skin was crawling. He said he couldn't wait to see me again.

He called several times. I finally programmed his number into my phone so that, every time he called, the word "FEET" flashed up on my cell phone as a warning.

Loneliness and self-pity are never the proper foundation for dating anyone for any reason whatsoever.

Loneliness

Family duties called, and I braced for a trip home. As I prepared for my trip, I tried to express how I was truly feeling to my best friend. I was having financial trouble for the first time in fifteen years, but that wasn't the source of my sadness. I was about to visit my family, but that wasn't the source of my sadness. In truth, I was lonely. I wanted someone to spoon with. I wanted someone to be alone together with. I wanted someone to kiss goodnight. I wanted someone who missed me when I was gone. I didn't think it was too much to ask for, but I didn't know how to get it. I didn't know how to tell my friends that was why I was so sad. Because I was often the source of strength, I didn't think they'd believe I had the same insecurities they did. Again, I cried. Was I so emotionally crippled that I'd never recover? Would I ever be able to honestly tell anyone the depth of my fears? If I cried when I felt love, did it scare people away? I feared the only solution was to do what I'd done so far. I spoke in half truths as I lay another brick on the wall.

I was feeling too vulnerable to spend alone time with my mother. I was sure that raging hormones and a trip home were a recipe for disaster. Even so, I tried to prepare for my trip. I needed to know who I was.

These are the qualities I see in myself: smart, happy, content, healthy, attractive, warm, and kind.

My friends tell me they see these qualities in me: smart, funny, secretive, healthy, beautiful, loving, and generous.

My whole life my mother has told me I am stupid, fat, unkempt, slothful, lazy, without achievement, and uncaring.

My Mother, My Self

I once went to the theater to see the most frightening movie I had ever seen. To this day, it brings chills. The thought of it brings up deep-seeded feelings of fear, hate, and terror. Although the film title is unassuming, I am not aware of anyone who might have seen it that was unmoved. For me, it was like seeing my deepest secrets on the screen for everyone to see. I was exposed. The movie was *Ordinary People*.

There in front of my eyes was the woman I am still afraid of becoming. Mary Tyler Moore somehow morphed into a seemingly coldhearted woman who was unable to express any emotion. In the throes of unspeakable family tragedy, she remained unwilling to bend, unwilling to express love or vulnerability. That was my fear. And that was my mother.

That was how I was nurtured and how I feared I would nurture others. It was the heart of why I decided that, before I even had sex, I would have no children. The fear that my children would feel as unloved as I did was enough to seal my fate. I vowed to never have children. Until those words were written on this page, I have never confessed that decision to anyone.

I have always been very wary of sharing my core. Those who love me may feel they already know me because of glimpses they have caught over the years, but how could they? My journey to the core of my being began as my menstrual cycle was ending. I am just now discovering what is buried behind the wall I have so carefully built. What I have seen through the microscope I have focused on myself has surprised even me. The unfolding of my new life seems to be a catalyst for brief glimpses of my past, of the moments that brought me here.

When I Grow Up

Some people have known what they wanted to do since they were small. They have a passion for music or science, a sense of belonging. When I was little, I wanted to be someone else.

I would watch old movies and want to be one of those happy people on the screen. I wanted to be Dorothy in the *Wizard of Oz*. I just never wanted to leave the Emerald City. I never understood why she'd leave that beautiful place where everyone sang just so she could go back home to Kansas. In fact, I still think the final lesson in the film is misplaced.

I wanted to be Pollyanna and create rainbows in people's homes. I wanted to have scathingly brilliant ideas. In fact, for a very long period, I thought that, if I tried hard enough, I could be Hayley Mills. When I was alone, I believed I was Hayley Mills.

When the astronauts went into outer space, I wanted to be with them. For hours, I'd sit in the middle of fields in North Dakota, waiting for aliens to come and pick me up. I hoped that if they were smart enough to get here, they would be smart enough to know who wanted to leave with them.

Truthfully, I just wanted to be somebody else. It drove me to want to be an actress later in life. It wasn't my love of the craft. I had never seen a play. I just wanted to be somebody different. I wanted to be somebody happy. I wanted to be somebody else. That's why I was good when I was performing. I went so far into my new self that I disappeared.

This escape from myself made giving up acting and singing difficult. I realized that being in a play didn't make me more loved. Singing in a band didn't make my mother appreciate my talent. Only once in college did my parents ever make the effort to see me perform. Now I realize that my years of angst, struggle, and trying for recognition were apparently for naught. My mother, the person whose love I was seeking, didn't even realize or care that any of it was going on.

My Mother's Eyes

On my last trip home, something happened that caused me to admit a terrible truth to myself. The mother I love and the mother I fear is the mother I loathe. We cannot have a conversation where I am not the stupid one. I am the one who is uncaring. I am the one who lies. I knew this brief trip home would be stressful, and I wasn't disappointed. My family is filled with damaged people. No one was happy. We had arguments over nothing in particular and no one ever said what we felt.

As my trip was ending, my mother and I were exchanging pleasantries that I felt came from the fact that I had bought food and left a check. During the course of her monologue regarding all of the stupid and annoying people she had known, she complained of the running toilet that had only made that racket since my arrival. She complained of the racket made by the people talking outside.

Since I lived in Manhattan, I told her I hadn't really noticed the noise. She asked what was wrong with me and complained that I must be hard of hearing. I decided to ignore it, so she pushed, telling me not to ignore her and asking what's wrong with me. I clearly needed to have my hearing tested. Against all better judgment, I decided to respond.

I told her that I did have minor hearing loss. Rather than express motherly concern, she told me that I was lying. She asked if I'd had some kind of test to describe it in detail. What do they do? What was the room like? I was momentarily stunned. I explained that I had hearing loss from singing in bands in my twenties. Her response was to call me a liar again. She told me that I never had a band. She said I made up more about myself than anyone she'd ever known.

I reminded her that my first ten years in New York were spent in pursuit of an acting and singing career. She told me that I was wrong. I looked her straight in the eye and asked her if she knew what I'd done with my life.

"You worked in Macy's," she said.

"No," I said.

She replied, "Well, you sold cosmetics."

"I did that for three months to help pay the rent," I said.

"Well, you worked at some law firm," she said.

I explained that I had more than one band. I sang backup and appeared in cabaret shows. I did extra work on television, and I was in an Off-Off-Broadway show. She said it couldn't be true because neither she nor my father knew about any of this. My father has been dead for years, so he's really not a good source for confirmation. We didn't discuss how accomplished I was in my last career in the legal industry. I don't know why, but I felt like bursting into tears.

The whole situation was absolutely ridiculous. A

fight over nothing was brewing. I realized this wasn't the moment for a confrontation. Despite that feeling, I told her that she was wrong. She told me that I was clearly a smart-mouthed know-it-all. An old wound was opened. I wasn't sure which one, but I just knew I felt small. I wanted to cry. I wanted to feel a loving hug. I wouldn't get it. I was feeling vulnerable.

I wanted desperately to call The Bartender. I knew I shouldn't. I feared that, if I did call him, he'd say no. In my heart, my mother's accusations were confirmed. I truly was unlovable. I was that sure The Bartender's arms were the only arms that could comfort me, but I was afraid to ask for them.

Suicide

The child of an acquaintance had a boyfriend commit suicide. She wondered if the same experience had an impact on how I loved. Of course it did. There was no way to avoid it. She just had to remember that the difference between our experiences was that I had never discussed my boyfriend's suicide with anyone, much less my mother. This child's mother was listening with open arms.

It had been more than thirty years. For some reason, I chose this moment to tell my mother that a friend had asked me to talk to this teenage girl and share our unique experience. My mother merely gave me a disapproving look. There was no discussion or concern over how I might feel about it. There was no discussion of the past. There was no discussion. Period. She merely lit a cigarette and turned up the television. It was another thing that apparently didn't happen.

I left my mother's house an hour before I needed to. She said good-bye, but there was no hug or kiss good-bye. She didn't tell me to have a safe trip. I cried all the way to the airport, only pulling myself together to return my rented car.

Two hours passed in the airport. I cried because I wanted to reach out to The Bartender. I decided not to call him. I wondered if this was strength and wisdom or foolish pride and stupidity. I wondered if I was doomed to repeat the mistakes made with my Drummer. What I did know is that this feeling came from a place of fear. I was terrified of asking the question and getting the response. I didn't want to be Mary Tyler Moore in *Ordinary People*. I didn't want to be my mother. Over these past few months, I couldn't be sure about how to gage my feelings. I wept bitterly all the way home.

The Bartender Returns

Freed from the shackles of my mother's house, I returned to New York. I was still sad and feeling small. Men from a variety of Internet dating sites had written to me, but I had no interest in starting another round. I didn't respond to any of them.

In a moment of weakness, I decided to reach out to The Bartender. Fearing rejection, I called in the evening when I knew he was at work. My intent was to leave a lighthearted message, only saying "Hello." Instead, at the mere sound of his voice on his outgoing message, I crumbled and left a tearful message telling him how I was sad and didn't know who else to call.

He called me early the next morning and offered to come to my rescue. As he crossed my threshold, we fell into each other's arms and made love for hours. He soothed me by telling me that I was all the things I hoped to be and that I was none of the things my mother claimed. His eyes were kind and loving, and he revealed another piece of his soul to me. We parted and agreed we shouldn't see each other again. We both knew we were lying, but we said it anyway.

Opera Man

In a brief attempt to forget The Bartender and move on, I agreed to meet a charming young man for yet another museum outing. He was just beginning an opera career and new to the city, so I decided to give him a tour of the Museum of Natural History. He called me as I was on my way to let me know he was there waiting for me. He admitted he was nervous about meeting me.

I arrived, and Opera Man was smiling broadly and waving from the top of the museum steps. He was absolutely adorable. We wandered through the museum for hours, chatting easily on our travels. When we arrived in the room of African peoples, he surprised me with a little kiss. I couldn't believe that this thirty-six-year-old man was making me blush.

It was clear as we left the museum that neither of us was ready to end our date, so I happily agreed to join him for a drink. We laughed and flirted with each other over a smart cocktail, then he kissed me again. It was time to leave the bar and we still weren't ready to go our separate ways so he asked me to a movie. We sat in the back row and kissed like we were in high school.

Opera Man is more than charming. He was smart and attentive and wanted to see me again. We planned another date for later that week and for a brief moment I forgot that The Bartender had chosen his other life rather than one with me.

Old Faithful

The funny thing about going through menopause is that you think you're home free. You may be getting hot flashes, but your menstrual cycle stops. Or so you think. I had gone for nearly eight months without a cycle. For my whole life, I had known when I was getting my period. I was so in tune with my cycle that I knew an hour before it would happen. I was never caught by surprise until now. There were no cramps or typical warnings.

At the end of our second date, I asked Opera Man up to my apartment for a drink. He kissed and touched me. Then, like a geyser, I exploded. There was no way to hide and no way to explain how I couldn't have known what was about to happen. It was as if the floodgates had opened.

Despite his youth, Opera Man was more adult about the situation than I was. He stayed with me, spooned me, and slept the night in my bed. It was very sweet. I couldn't understand how I could get such tenderness from a virtual stranger and not from the man I seemed to have foolishly given my heart to. I cried softly, and Opera Man comforted me. He had no idea that I was shedding my tears for another man.

The Bartender Continues

His father was sick. As The Bartender was preparing for his own dysfunctional trip home, this time he reached out to me. He was more vulnerable than usual and his vulnerability allowed me to expose more of myself. I was more open with him than I had ever been with myself. Not only was there absolute abandon in our lovemaking, but with our emotions. I know the intent of the tryst was to say good-bye yet again, but it felt more like a doomed hello.

At that moment, I knew I was in love with him. I didn't say the words, but I knew it was true. I asked him what he wanted. He said he didn't want anything to change. I was wounded to the core, but I didn't say the words. I wanted him to always be by my side. I needed him to never leave me. I felt most like myself in his arms. Again, he couldn't see his way clearly to do what would make him happy. I couldn't see a way to continue being the other woman.

He told me he was leaving to visit his family. I knew it would be more traumatic than my little jaunt home. I didn't know if he was going by himself or with her. All I knew is that I wasn't invited. Once again, he left my side, but it was different this time. He vowed to come back to me and to think about his situation and the state of his life.

Getting in Shape

As the days grew warmer and longer, I made a pact with my girlfriends to power walk every morning. We were determined. We would have divinely toned bodies. I knew that fifty was now merely a year away and the support of these women would help in my quest to be more like Tina Turner by my next birthday. I made a vow to myself that, by the time my forty-ninth birthday arrived, I would be in such good form that I could begin to secretly sing and dance in heels in my apartment to "Proud Mary" each morning to supplement my walk. I vowed to have legs like Tina's within the year.

The first walks were difficult. All things considered, I'm sure that sex is a much better workout. Sex builds strength, and it's good for the heart and skin. Sex stops my hot flashes. I could go on and on, but, most importantly, I never mind doing it. At any given moment, I am happily ready for a workout. The same cannot be said for my power walks.

The First Real Date

The Bartender called me from the road. He asked how I was. I lied and said I was fine. He told me of his woes and how sad he was. Although I was feeling angry and betrayed by his inability to love me, I listened and gave solace.

Discussions with The Bartender took a turn. He was sharing more intimate details of his life, his past, and his desires. I was feeling bolder, but there was still a distance. Now that I had admitted to myself that I was actually in love, it actually physically hurt me. It made me want to cry and to wring my hands in despair. I know The Bartender is conflicted. Clearly, so am I.

He called me several times from home, and we were both anxious for his return. When The Bartender returned, he called me. We planned to meet for a lunch date. We were actually going to meet in public in the neighborhood he worked and lived in. The thought of this first date made me feel hopeful.

It was hot outside, and I dressed in crisp white linen, showing off my tan. We met on the street, and he greeted me with a kiss hello. He told me how beautiful I looked and kissed me again. We talked about the difficulty of our relationship. Even so, we were on a date, and I was happy. In the restaurant, we held hands and looked into each other's eyes, searching for some kind of answer. The Bartender didn't seem to have any answers for me, and I felt hurt.

I had lost my appetite so we decided to leave the restaurant for a walk through Central Park. He took me down a path I didn't know. He grabbed me and kissed me. We were getting so carried away that it was clear that we had to have each other so we hailed a cab to take us to my apartment. On the way, he stopped at his apartment to get work clothes so he could be with me as long as possible. We arrived at my home, and we couldn't keep our hands and mouths off each other.

As he got ready to leave for work, we made plans for the following day. Another date. He selected a place he loved.

The Second Date

We planned to meet in front of his favorite museum. I was excited about our second date, so I arrived a bit early. The day was lovely, so I waited outside on the museum steps. The Bartender walked up and greeted me with a kiss. We went inside to peruse the art. We were holding hands, laughing, and touching each other. After an hour, we decided to leave the museum. He announced he had some errands to run. I was wounded. An hour! I only got one hour.

We walked down the street with his arm around me. I was clearly upset. He hugged me, and I burst into tears. I wasn't good at being vulnerable. He said he'd walk me to work, but my eyes were swollen from crying. We sat on the stoop of a brownstone, and he comforted me. He told me how much he cared for me. He said he didn't deserve me.

I looked at him and pointed out that he surely must know that I was falling for him. He didn't say, "I love you, too." He just looked into my eyes. Neither of us could break the gaze.

For the first time in my life, I decided I was feeling brave enough to tell a grown man that I was in love with him. I surprised myself by staying calm. It wasn't a happy or loving moment. We had been on the verge of breaking up yet again. I somehow knew it wouldn't be responded to in kind, but I had to tell him anyway.

I didn't cry or gasp for breath. My heart didn't stop pounding.

I simply told him and then held his gaze. I saw love and remorse at the same time in his eyes. He didn't say, "I love you, too." He instead confessed a deep wound in his soul that I'm sure only a few knew about. It was a wound so deep that it hurt me to see it opened. We continued to talk and coo, and I finally had to go to work.

We talked regularly. He said he missed me. He cared for me. He worried about me. He said he prayed for me. We talked about when we'd get to see each other again. Even so, I could feel it coming. It was like a vise tightening around my heart. I easily burst into tears. I was sure that telling The Bartender I loved him was the right thing to do. It is what was in my heart, but I had no precedent. I didn't know how to say it or how to gauge the reaction.

We made plans to see each other again in two days.

My Heart Is Breaking

The following day, I was out for a smart cocktail with friends when The Bartender called. I was happy to hear from him and assumed he was calling to confirm our date for the following day. The conversation started innocently enough with a funny story. We laughed together and talked about our pending date. Then he said it.

"I don't think I can go on."

"What do you mean?"

"I can't see you anymore."

I told him he was cruel to even start this conversation on the phone when he knew we couldn't finish it. Harsh words were spoken. He was wounded. I was crushed.

He was stomping on my heart.

He said, "I can't talk anymore. I'm too upset."

"He's too upset," I thought. *"Is he kidding?"*

Who was delivering the blows? He hung up the phone, and I cried. I wonder if he was crying alone in his room. I didn't know I could feel this way. I pulled myself together and rejoined my friends.

The next morning, he called to apologize for

being so angry on the phone. I was afraid of losing him. The Bartender knew I was worried and scared, so he came over just to be with me and hold me. He wanted to be near me just because he knew I needed him there. We held each other. Then he made love to me in a way that was sweet and somehow filled with anger.

When he left, I cried.

Breaking Up Is Hard To Do

It was time. We made a date to break up. It was unspoken, but I knew. We had been down this road before, but never with such conviction. The Bartender looked sad as he crossed my threshold. We both knew that harsh words would be spoken and both of our hearts would break that day.

He said he wasn't choosing her over me.

But he didn't stay.

He said he needed to put out one fire before starting another.

But the fire was already burning.

He was wounded when I suggested he didn't really care. He was wounded, and he cried.

But he didn't stay.

We had breakup sex. Then we made love. I wept bitterly as I had an orgasm. Then he cried and held me.

But he didn't stay.

We were complete in each other's arms.

But he didn't stay.

He left and I wept. I shouldn't have, but I called him as he left my building. He said it was too hard to say good-bye again.

He said he didn't want to leave me.

But he didn't stay.

He didn't want to hurt me.

But he didn't stay.

The echoes of my cries filled the room until I fell asleep. I woke up exhausted and listened to the message he left saying how much he cared for me. The message he left saying how it hurt him to see me cry.

But he didn't stay.

I cried all day. I cried into the night. I expected he'd wait and give me a rest, but he called the next morning to see how I was doing. I cried bitterly to myself. I shocked my best friend by crying bitterly to her. She was comforting and kind, but she was unsure about what to do for me. I was hurt and stunned when she said she wasn't angry with him. I was unable to talk through my tears. She thought he was doing the right thing by waiting, gaining distance, becoming whole, becoming free, and leaving me.

Recovery

I feared I was setting myself up for abuse. I was feeling more than reckless. I spied Relocation Man online and, looking for solace, decided to drop him a line. He was kind and wanted to meet. We made a date. I knew it was the wrong thing to do. So did he. We planned to meet on the coming Monday. I cried myself to sleep throughout the weekend.

Monday arrived and he didn't call. He offered no explanation. I was so angry that I wrote to him and told him how I felt. I spewed bitter words meant not for him but for The Bartender.

New men made contact on the Internet, and I was blocking them from all angles. Because my heart was broken, I contemplated taking risks that I never thought I'd even consider, but I really wasn't up for anymore rounds of dating at the moment. Instead, I stayed in the safety of my home and lost myself in work.

The One-Year Mark

It was really quite amazing that I had hit the one-year mark. It was one year of musings and one year closer to fifty. The last year had gone by so quickly. In the blink of an eye, I had a sexual awakening, brushed against my fear of mortality, came to terms with the fact that my body and my mind were on separate courses, and, probably most profoundly, exposed my soft inner being for the first time in years. I exposed myself enough that I have been overwhelmed by the fullness of my own heart as well as the knowledge of how it could break. I knew I could survive both.

My hormones were still out of whack. I awaited the results of yet another blood test from doctors to confirm what I already knew. I was careening into menopause.

Now that I had hit this one-year landmark, I felt compelled to examine my progress. When I began, I felt afraid and sure at the same time. Looking back, I thought the driving force was anger. I was angry with the unfairness of the world. I was angry because I didn't have a penis of my own or otherwise. I was angry over the breakup of my last long-term relationship, the one with my job. I was angry because I thought I had no love in my life. I was angry at the world and with myself.

Some of those feelings were legitimate; others were entirely misplaced. I had spent so much time in an emotional shutdown that I was afraid of even letting me see what was inside. I suppose I had some idea what lurked on the inside of the walls I had carefully built around myself. Even so, I hadn't so much as peeked inside the walls for so long that I feared what I might find there.

The Real Lesson Learned

The only person who truly doesn't see the value in my love is me. Throughout the last year, I blamed my display of emotion on my raging hormones. That was only partially true. I still cried every day. In fact, I am crying as I write this, but I don't think I can blame all of my tears on hormones. Some of my tears are good.

No, that wasn't true. All of my tears were good. Perhaps it was because I was more comfortable in my own skin. This was a function of my weight loss and an acceptance of myself. I was heartbroken. I had been heartbroken for years for a variety of reasons. Only now was it exposed. Only now did I attempt to share my pain with others.

I discovered that none of my friends ever thought I was perfect. It was me who tried to present that image. They just never told me I was naked, which was really a testament to their love. Now that I was sharing my vulnerability with them, they were standing there with me.

I realized that the feeling they weren't entirely supportive came not from them, but from the newness for me. I still needed more kudos, hugs, and an understanding of the fact that I didn't even know how deep the water was. My friends needed to be patient and wait before my anchor hit bottom.

I also learned through the pain of my broken heart that as well as the support of my friends, I was truly blessed and happy. I was so happy that I felt beauty in small moments that I would have rushed by a year ago.

I was on my roof deck on a beautiful afternoon and I let the colors wash over me. Somewhere below the clump of trees that held back the river, a train rumbled slowly by, its lonesome whistle filtering through the branches. The sun was getting lower in the sky, making the river, the bridge, and the cars rushing across shimmer like silver foil. Only the white speck of a boat sailing by cut the water. The sun was beating down, warming my body, but the wind from the river was cold against my skin. Even my glass of water tasted good. Everything surrounding me was beautiful. I should have gone downstairs to add some more clothing, but I didn't want to miss how the light would change the colors in the sky with each moment. Everything that touched my senses was as beautiful as my memory of Christmas lights as a child.

My Birthday

It was my birthday, and I knew The Bartender would leave me high and dry. If I didn't hear from him, I'd be devastated. If I did hear from him, I'd be devastated. There was just no way around it.

The day before my birthday, I was on the phone with my best friend, making plans for the big day. As we were talking, the doorman rang up to say I had a package downstairs. It was unusual that he didn't send the delivery person up, so I told my best friend I'd call her back once I went down to collect my birthday surprise.

The Bartender had hand-delivered my present and then run away. I read the card and melted into a pool of tears. He wrote beautiful words and signed the card, "With love." I was inconsolable. I couldn't even read the words over the phone to my girlfriend.

Later in the day, I called him to thank him for the present. He came all that way to deliver it.

"Why didn't you say hello or give it to me in person?" I asked.

"I don't know," he said. "When I arrived, I panicked and decided to go back home."

My girlfriend came over to console me and help me celebrate my birthday. I realized that love came from all around me.

Mr. Right Name

I returned to the Internet to search for the love of my life. I revised my on-line dating profile and said as much and waited to see who would respond. It was interesting that, with the exception of yet another beautiful man who was too young, the men of interest who had been contacting me all had the same name as The Bartender. Two handsome, creative, employed, age-appropriate men had called. They left messages. Each time, I shuddered as I heard them say their name. The name was right. It was just the wrong voice on the other end of the phone.

I agreed to meet one of them for a drink. I arrived at the bar, and Mr. Right Name was actually more attractive than his dating profile photo. While he was rather charming, I couldn't get past the fact that just two blocks away the other man with the same name was tending another bar. I was distracted. I tried to be charming, but I knew that I was occasionally not there. We had a nice conversation and then walked a few blocks together before parting ways. We gave each other a little peck good-bye as he said he'd like to do it again. Then he hugged me. It was a real hug. I hugged him back and felt soothed. He said he'd call me the next week.

As I walked away from him, I didn't look back. I wondered if he looked back at me.

I was feeling more than sorry for myself. Because I couldn't call The Bartender, I stopped on the way home to buy a secret stash of bagels for carb-loading. Bread is like crack for me. After one taste, I couldn't be stopped. Within twelve hours of saying goodnight to Mr. Right Name, I had eaten two bagels, two bialys, and some pork fried rice. I was on a downward spiral. I lacked the courage to throw out the remaining two bagels. Instead, I stashed them in my freezer for an emergency fix.

I was a mess. As I stuffed my face with bagels, I looked up The Bartender's number on my cell phone at least fifty times. I didn't press Send. Just below his name was Mr. Right Name. I saw their names side by side and cried each time. I desperately wanted to call The Bartender. It had been nearly two weeks since our last contact, and I was feeling more than sorry for myself.

I decided to put down the phone and write to Mr. Right Name, thanking him for the drink and a lovely end to my day. To my surprise, he wrote back, suggesting we get together again and even go to the theater. It was a real date. Perhaps he'd turn out to be Mr. Right after all.

Health

I went for my annual physical three months late. My doctor placed regular calls to goad me into coming. Feeling betrayed by The Bartender, I had already been to my gynecologist to be tested for every STD known to mankind. With the confirmation I was HIV-free, I decided my doctor could find no worse fate. I agreed to see him for a physical.

The good doctor politely began his usual litany of questions, "How are you?"

I immediately burst into tears and told him I had broken up with my boyfriend. I even confessed I knew The Bartender was unavailable to begin with. I let the doctor know I had just passed all of my STD testing with flying colors. As I blew my nose and dabbed away tears, he suggested that my hormone levels be scrutinized. While I could stand to lose another ten pounds, he found that I was incredibly healthy. Despite that, he reminded me that fifty was coming and I should begin to prepare myself for the benchmark tests that came along with that.

The summer was sweltering, and I was feeling fat and bloated. The pact I formed with my girlfriends to power walk every morning had been good for my cardio fitness. I just needed to try to lose a little weight. But I was self-medicating myself with carbohydrates.

Bread was my worst enemy. I had successfully given up cigarettes, and now I only drank coffee as a special treat. I still drank scotch. My problem was bread. If you give me a slice, I'll eat a loaf. You can add fat of any kind: butter, margarine, cream cheese, or olive oil. It doesn't really matter. I could live on nothing but bread and water. I never really understood the whole thing about the cruelty of giving prisoners only bread and water. I'd be in my own special, lethargic, fat heaven.

I must stop the madness. When I grow up, I want to be like Tina Turner. I want to be one of the hottest, non-surgically altered fifty-year-old women who ever existed. I must rededicate myself to fitness, but just like The Bartender, I was finding it difficult to commit.

Mr. Right Name Returns

My heart had been broken, but I seemed to have survived. I had cried uncountable tears and eaten more carbohydrates than anyone should be allowed, but I had survived.

As I contemplated what the next chapter in my life would be, my phone rang. To my surprise, Mr. Right Name was on the other end of the phone. His persistence flattered me. Because I hadn't responded to his emails, he had decided to call to tell me he'd like to see me again. We chatted easily, and I agreed to meet him for a movie.

The date night arrived, and I surprised myself at how excited I was that this kind and handsome man wanted to date me. I took special care in getting ready for our date. I got up early in the morning and went out for a manicure and pedicure. I ate something sensible for lunch. Then I showered and perused my closet for a suitable outfit.

I put on a simple skirt and T-shirt. Because Mr. Right Name wasn't that much taller than I was, I took care to select shoes that weren't too high. I was having a good hair day and feeling confident. When I arrived at the theater, he was waiting out front with tickets in hand. He greeted me with a sweet kiss hello.

I happily agreed to join him for a drink after the movie, and we walked a few blocks to one of his favorite haunts. He smiled broadly as we walked through the door of a charming little neighborhood joint and took seats at the bar. Mr. Right Name was clearly a regular, and he introduced me to the bartender and a few of the regular clientele. After a couple hours of talking with his neighborhood buddies, his phone rang. He explained that it was his ex-wife, and he excused himself to take the call.

He came back, looking a bit annoyed and panicked at the same time. His ex lived two blocks from him, and they shared custody of the child and a dog. While I didn't quite understand the specifics, he unexpectedly had to walk the dog, who had apparently been left with Mr. Right Name's doorman.

He paid the bill at the bar, and I joined him on the walk to his apartment to retrieve the dog. He told me that he'd like to take the dog up to the apartment before putting me in a cab. Because I had to go to the bathroom and I was dying to see his place, I agreed.

The apartment was immaculate. I don't believe I have ever been in any place so tidy and exacting in my entire life.

I asked, "Did you hire a decorator?"

He proudly announced how he had done the apartment himself and discussed his combination of texture and fabrics in the different rooms. I excused myself and went to the bathroom. Even the seashells on the counter were arranged in perfect little motifs. I really didn't know what to make of it.

After years of living in Manhattan, I had extremely sophisticated gaydar. In all my years, I had never discussed swatches with a straight man. There had been no other telltale signs. Surprised, I didn't know what to think. Had the experience in Catholic school made him take cleanliness being next to godliness too seriously? Had I discovered the secret reason for his divorce?

He walked me out of the apartment to hail me a cab. As he opened the door to the car and just before I got in, he grabbed me and kissed me hard. Perhaps I had overreacted to his domestic skills. I rode home in the cab, vowing to not dial his number but to wait to see if he'd call again.

Success

It had been about a year since I started dating. Once again, I was date-free on a Saturday night. This time last year, I had received my first Valentine's present from a man since high school. I had also received jewelry from the same man on my birthday. Despite the circumstances, I knew it was a move in the right direction. I really wanted a man to be with me for the New Year. I really wanted Thanksgiving even more than I wanted Christmas, but I felt I shouldn't be greedy. Ringing in the New Year with someone other than myself would be a first.

I had survived. A couple friends from my old life had fallen by the wayside. I still reached out to them. I didn't fault them for not calling back. I knew how unhappy they were even if they didn't. I knew they might never again be able to bear the sight of me in my joyful state, but I'd leave my door open should they ever need to come in.

When I began my journey, I was working without a net and unsure if I could survive. What surprised me the most was my new definition of success. I was confident. Financially, I was a wreck. That wouldn't be true for long, but my financial worth used to be what defined me. It was certainly how I thought my family and friends defined me. Now it was the success of my friends, the number of times I laughed in a day, and the number of people who embraced my faults.

At last, I was truly successful.

Lady Stetson

As I was checking messages one afternoon, I heard a familiar voice from the past. I was floored. The Athlete had pursued me more than a year ago. We had exchanged brief histories, photos, and phone numbers. At one point, we were even to meet for a drink, but life got in the way. It just never happened, and I confess that I hadn't given him another thought. Apparently, the same was not true for him.

I went to my computer and searched for photos and profiles of tall, former professional ballplayers. He said he was six-foot-three, and the photo was quite handsome. When we finally made phone contact again, he explained there had been many changes in his life over the last year and he had remembered our conversations fondly. He wanted to reconnect. Typically, I'd refuse to meet for more than a cup of coffee or a smart cocktail at a first meeting, but the Athlete promised dinner at a fine establishment in Manhattan that I'd wanted to try. I couldn't resist the promise of fine dining, so I said yes.

Date day arrived and I was looking forward to it. I was having a good hair day and despite the past year's indulgences, I looked great in my black suit and silk blouse. Since the Athlete claimed to be six-foot-three, I was happily wearing heels. I arrived a bit early, took a seat at the bar, and ordered a glass of wine.

I lost track of time as I sipped my tasty glass of wine and read my book. The staff was eyeing me, and I suddenly realized that I had been sitting there for thirty minutes. I had never waited that long for anyone, not for a business appointment, not for a friend, and certainly not for a date with someone I'd never met before. I immediately asked for my check.

As I was paying my bill and preparing to leave the restaurant, a tall man came rushing in, placed a shopping bag on the barstool next to me, and ran off to the men's room. A couple minutes later, he reappeared, apologizing profusely and blaming the traffic for his tardiness. While the man before me was six-foot-three, that was the only recognizable thing about him. The Athlete was awkward and unattractive.

Once we were seated, the waiter brought over a plate of complimentary snacks. The Athlete lowered his head and began shoveling them in his mouth at an unbelievable rate. I couldn't believe I had been foolish enough to agree to dine with a complete stranger.

Between bites that no human could ever take, he insisted I open his gift. The first item was a bag of candy kisses. If he had been taking seemingly human bites, I might have found his line about later sharing a few kisses charming, but the thought of possibly kissing that mouth exploding with food repulsed me. As I opened the remainder of the gift, I couldn't believe my eyes. The Athlete had presented me with a gift set of Lady Stetson. I don't believe I had even seen a bottle of Lady Stetson since the 1980s. I was suddenly struck by the ridiculous notion that he was a crazy man who lured women home, enticing them with bottles of drugstore perfume that he had stashed in his closet for the last twenty years.

As dinner proceeded, the Athlete became louder and more forceful. The staff, clearly becoming as concerned as I, monitored the table more closely and constantly refilled my water glass while giving me pitying glances. At one point, the Athlete tried to feed me. I politely said no. He continued to attempt to feed me until I found it necessary to shout out a forceful, "No!" The waiters circled around the table, like wagons in the Westerns I had watched on television as a child.

I couldn't get out of there fast enough and back to the safety of the streets of New York City. I felt like the cab driver was the cavalry riding me home. Perhaps the gift of Lady Stetson was appropriate after all.

A New Beginning

School was about to start. Autumn has always felt like a new beginning for me with crispness and the smell of new crayons in the air.

Once again, The Bartender reappeared to break my heart. When we last broke up, I told him that there were two reasons he could contact me: if he were truly single and ready to pursue a relationship with me or if he had decided to marry and spend the rest of his life with his other woman. I thought I deserved that courtesy. So, when he called and asked to see me, I foolishly thought he had come back to me because he had made a decision to change his path.

During this same time, Hurricane Katrina was blowing into New Orleans. My family lives there and I was terrified. The Bartender remained by my side. He was with me the moment I discovered that, while my mother refused to leave, my baby sister had safely left the Crescent City. The relief was so great that I wept in The Bartender's arms and I was beyond happy that he was there for me.

When he left that day, it was finally over. He wasn't coming back to be with me. He merely came back to break my heart one last time. I know he was hurt as well and I was glad for it. We both cried bitterly this time when it was over. Even so, I still hoped he would someday see his way clear to be with me.

Don't judge me harshly. I admit I still wanted him in spite of everything. I loved him. I was less than a year from my fiftieth birthday and believed the feeling of happiness he gave me when we were together was worth being made a fool over.

It didn't matter.

He didn't stay.

I was heartbroken.

I cried every day.

So Many Lessons Learned

I found that I could confront my fears and survive their wrath. I was no longer afraid to show my tremendous capacity to love. I was also no longer afraid of being loved. I wasn't afraid of the rejection when my love was shunned. My heart was broken, but it didn't kill me.

Now that I didn't have The Bartender's body, my hot flashes continued on a daily basis. The shift in hormones over the last year seemed to have made me more emotional and vulnerable, but I once again seemed to have focus. I was multitasking again, and business was beginning to pick up. I was finding other places to share my heart. I had begun to work on charities and finding great joy in it.

For the moment, I thought I was done with surfing the Internet for men. The Bartender still had my heart, but I was willing to offer it up to another honorable man should one actually cross my path. I realized my growth came from within, but I also realized The Bartender was the catalyst for much of my growth. For that, I thank him. For that reason, I wrote the following love letter to him, even though I didn't send it.

A Love Letter

I love you. I love your mind. I love your imperfect body when it is with my imperfect body and how we fit together perfectly. I love how you cry at injustice. I love how you make me feel about myself. I love how my heart opens when I am with you. I love how when are bodies are pressed against each other we cannot distinguish our heartbeats.

I love how it feels to take down the bricks one by one when I am with you. I love that you have helped me to be less fearful about exposing myself. What is most difficult for me is that you clearly don't love me with the same breadth. I thought you did. I even believed you told me you did. I was wrong, but I am better for having loved and lost. To tell the truth, I still hold out hope that you'll discover how much you miss me. I hope you will learn about me what I have learned about myself.

I am a woman to be reckoned with. I am a woman whose love is so powerful that it can be scary, but that love can form a protective shield around you. I may not get you in the end, but I will love you forever. I believe I have found what makes me happy, and that is you. I believe I make you happy too.

'Tis the Season Again

The year had flown by. My hot flashes were running rampant. It was the dead of winter and I was sweating as I walked down the street. The thought of Christmas shopping in crowded stores was overwhelming. Unless I could purchase it on the Internet and have it delivered on time for Christmas, there would be no presents under my tree this year.

My friends and their families would be joining me for both Thanksgiving and Christmas dinner. I love hosting the holiday meals, and I love to be surrounded by the people I love and who love me. It had become a tradition, and I looked forward to the holidays each and every year. There could be no better way to tend to my broken heart.

I was happily preparing for the holidays with shopping, cooking, and going to holiday parties. I felt like I was ready to move on and reclaim my life. Festivities were under way and I was feeling happy, but the lack of sex made my hot flashes come more frequently. I was self-medicating with carbohydrates, but I was feeling good.

Then The Bartender called. He called on

Thanksgiving and again on Christmas. Each time I was hopeful that he was calling to say he was coming for dinner, but that wasn't the case. He just called without any purpose or thought. Each time, I was left with an aching so deep inside that I didn't know what to do with it.

I wasn't going to get what I wanted for Christmas this year. So much for happy holidays.

True Confession

In an effort to reclaim my favorite haunt in the New Year, I began to return to the bar on evenings I knew The Bartender wouldn't be working. Each time, I ended up in a flood of tears.

A part of me wanted to call his home number and tell *her* about me so she would be as heartbroken as me. I looked at his number on my cell phone every day and resisted hitting Send. I thought about calling his home number when I knew he was at work so I could hear how *her* voice sounded. I wanted to know what it was that made him want to hear *her* voice before he slept and when he woke.

I cried every day after he left me. The calls during the holiday season left me more than wounded for Valentine's Day. I cried every waking minute that day. I probably shouldn't have done it, but I sent an e-card to The Bartender on that day. Part of me was looking for a finale. Part of me was looking to have him back in my bedroom.

I found myself staring at the computer screen, letting the words flow from my heart through my fingertips. Forgetting my head, I shared those words with him. I admitted I still wanted him despite everything.

I had no idea what I expected the response to my Valentine to be, but it wasn't the response I got.

I wanted to know how he was.

I wanted to know how he was doing at school.

I wanted to know how his family was doing.

I wanted to know if he was happy.

I wanted to know if he felt loved.

I sent him a long note telling him so and foolishly included my secret love letter to him. He wrote back to answer the questions he could and told me he hadn't made the decision to leave.

He told me he loved me.

He told me he cherished our time together.

He told me that my love was intimidating.

Enough.

The Scotsman

I had cried enough. I resolved to move on. I logged back on to the Internet dating sites, searching for a man. I discovered a charming Scotsman had sent emails asking to meet me for a drink. He was attractive, charming, and attentive. After our first date, he made it clear that he was available for a relationship. He called or sent me an email every day. My heart wasn't quite in it, but I agreed to meet him for a second date.

We had a lovely time over dinner. The Scotsman drew me out, and I told him that I was heartbroken. He wanted to know if I was truly ready for a relationship and I told him I that was. I wanted to be ready but I felt myself on the verge of tears as I told the Scotsman this lie.

He kissed me goodnight, and we made plans to see each other again. A few days later, I sent him an email telling him that I wasn't as ready as I thought I was. I never saw him or heard from him again.

The Architect

Soon after the Scotsman, I was surprised at my attraction to an age-appropriate man. The Architect's Internet profile was brief and to the point, but laced with humor. His photo was quite handsome. After a very quick email exchange, we chatted on the phone and agreed to meet for a drink.

We met at a lovely spot in Greenwich Village. I arrived before he did and wondered if he'd be as handsome as he was in his photo. Just as that thought crossed my mind The Architect walked in the door of the restaurant and I wasn't disappointed. He was a bit older and more disheveled than he was in the online photo but his unruly hair somehow added to his charm.

We talked easily for a couple hours. He seemed open about where he was in his life. He was very recently divorced. I found him to be quite charming, although his constant fidgeting and rearranging of items on the bar, combined with his middle-aged obsession with athletic competition, made me wonder if he had a bit of OCD. In any event, I agreed to let him drive me home, and we made plans for another date a few days later.

Our second date was brunch. Again, we chatted easily and talked of future plans to get together. The Architect walked me home, and I invited him up for tea. It was very civilized. He sat on the opposite side of the room and offered to do a couple things around the house. This was clearly the reaction of a man who had been married for a long time. I definitely found him attractive, but he was going to have to work at lighting my fire.

Just as it was time to say good-bye, he took me by surprise. He didn't just kiss me good-bye. He grabbed me and kissed me hard. I was surprised, but I kissed him back and enjoyed it. It wasn't just a kiss good-bye. We made out like teenagers for quite a while. Sadly, he had to leave to go to work for an important business meeting. I was surprised I think we were both left a bit breathless.

I was excited that our third date was to be on a Saturday night and I hoped we'd finish what was started in our little make out session after brunch. The Architect called before his arrival and said he had a sports injury. We were to go to an art exhibit, but, when he arrived, it was clear that he could barely walk. Instead, we went out for dinner. We considered taking a walk, but that obviously wasn't going to happen either. Whatever it was we had started after brunch wouldn't be finished after dinner. We discussed plans to get together again and I was getting excited about dating this grown-up man. I confess that I wasn't sure if I really liked him or if I just really wanted to like him.

Over the next couple weeks, the Architect and I talked on the phone several times, attempting to make plans. It became apparent that we both really wanted to make a go of it, but we really just didn't like each other that much. We both just stopped trying.

A Little Perspective

While I was trying to find out whether or not dating could mend a broken heart, true sorrow confronted me. One of my best friends in the world called to let me know that his partner wasn't expected to live more than a few weeks. I was stunned. Cancer had attacked his young body for only a few short months. It was untenable that he could lose his battle so quickly. I realized how much love they had for each other and how tragic it was that their love would be ripped from this physical world.

Within days of that initial call, my friend called to let me know that his partner had died. My heart broke for them both, and I made plans to visit him in Provincetown, Massachusetts.

When I arrived, I was overwhelmed. This time, my hormones weren't the cause for my tears. The living room had been converted into a bedroom and was filled with reminders of death. We worked hard to remove medical supplies and to bring some beautiful reminders of his partner's young life back into the room. The great love that lived there pushed back the sorrow of loss. I struggled to be strong as I filled my visit with cooking, cleaning, and hugs.

I could only stay for a couple days on this trip, but I kissed my friend good-bye and promised to return in two weeks for the memorial service. It wasn't until I was on the road again on my long drive home that I was overwhelmed. I burst into tears and cried for at least half of my seven-hour drive home.

I cried for the tragedy of a life lost so young.

I cried for my friend's loneliness.

I cried from sheer exhaustion.

I cried because I wanted to be in love.

I cried because I was afraid of loss.

I cried over the beauty of the love I had just witnessed.

Two weeks later, I returned for the memorial. The service was beautiful, filled with words of love, beautiful music and art. The following day I was able to secrete away with my friend and a few other people to a beautiful spot where we spread his love's ashes. We cried and hugged each other.

Here's the real lesson learned, the lesson we all need to strive to keep in our hearts and minds: There is no greater force in the universe than love.

California Dream

While I had been building walls around me to help me deal with the witness of grief, a beautiful man was calling me to see how I was doing.

A few weeks before my trip to Provincetown a very handsome man sent me a lovely email. I was more than disappointed to discover he was in California. I didn't think either of us thought about it, but he was kind and gentle. He was also fun to talk to. He came out of nowhere.

I feared I wouldn't be able to remain strong for my friend. I could feel the mortar hardening between the bricks as I lay the walls that would protect me on my visits. Each time I lay a new brick California Dream would be on the other end of my phone, taking the brick away. When I'd feel blue, like magic, my phone would ring. We were clearly growing fond of each other. I didn't know what to make of it, but I looked forward to each and every one of his calls and emails.

The Birth Festival

For as long as I can remember, I have been celebrating birth festivals rather than birthdays. Being a summer baby, friends have always been gone for my birthday so I decided to go for all the gusto. At first, I decided my birthday should last a full month. As I got older, I extended that time so my birth festival lasted from one month before and went straight through one month beyond the actual day. For my Fiftieth Birth Festival I decided to celebrate the entire year.

A big part of the celebration was to reunite with three dear friends I'd known since I first moved to New York. Around the time of September 11, 2001, these three girlfriends who lived in England and I agreed that we'd begin saving for our fiftieth birthday bash. We'd known each other since we were twenty-one. While we had remained in touch over the years, September 11 was the catalyst for us to stay even closer in touch. Our get-together would be a week of partner-free, child-free silliness that would celebrate that this year each of us would be hitting the half-century mark.

After much planning, we decided a date around

the midpoint of our birthdays would be most appropriate. We chose the week before Easter. New York is lovely in the spring. Imagine four perimenopausal women sharing a New York City apartment for a week. The conversations went from memories of years gone by to the sharing of hormonal surges and hot flashes.

Each one of us had taken very different life paths. Even so, we spent the week rediscovering all we had in common. We spent our days and nights dining and attending the theater. We discussed families, loss, aches and pains, joys, and heartbreak. We talked about wrinkles, facial hair, hormones, and hot flashes.

On the last night of our precious week together, we braved a trip to the lovely restaurant where The Bartender worked for dinner. Despite the fact that so many months had passed since our last encounter, of course my girlfriends wanted a peek at the man who had broken my heart.

We spent a tremendous amount of time dressing, primping, and then dressing again after hot flashes. Finally, we were ready for our entrance. We took a cab to the scene of the crime. When we walked in my party and I were immediately directed to a lovely table. I was sure The Bartender noticed me walk in, and I know my friends all took him in. Dinner was lovely, and we thoroughly enjoyed our meals. I surprised myself at how well I did at seeing him again. I was fine. I had a nice time and I was able to forget that he was behind the bar.

At some point before dessert was served, I excused myself to go to the ladies' room. Careful not to take notice of the bar, I made sure I was looking my best as I started my strut across the restaurant. I felt more than confident. As I approached the restroom, I had to squeeze by the crowd that was in that particular corner of the restaurant. As I squeezed past the men's room, the door flew open. Out stepped The Bartender. I might have audibly gasped. I confess I had never been so close to another human being without actually touching.

He spoke, "Hello."

"Hello," I said.

"You look terrific," he said.

"Thank you."

Then there was a long, awkward pause.

I stepped away and slipped into the ladies room. I suddenly no longer had the need to pee, but I made sure that my breathing was easy and I looked good before stepping back out into the restaurant. I moved back to the table and explained the incident. It was uncomfortable, but I seemed to be fine.

Later that night as I climbed into my bed alone I burst into tears. What was it? Was it sense memory, or was I still an open wound after so many months? One of my girlfriends came into my room because she could hear my sobs. I was inconsolable and I cried myself to sleep.

When my girlfriends went home to London, I was lonely for weeks. I had become used to the noise, to having someone to share a cup of coffee with me in the morning. When they left, my apartment was as empty as I think it had ever been. I had rambled around my large apartment for years on my own, and I had been fine with it. This was just a cruel reminder that I was truly lonely.

California Dream

My company was gone. The Bartender was gone. The Architect just faded away.

As the weeks passed, California Dream continued to call and send lovely messages. Our conversations were easy and always left me with a warm and happy feeling.

One evening, I returned from a night on the town with friends to discover an email message from him, letting me know he had booked a flight to visit and then gone straight to bed. I had a moment of excitement, which led to a moment of absolute panic. I couldn't believe that I couldn't call him. I was awake all night, having hot flashes in rapid succession. In the morning, he called. We discussed the wisdom of and our mutual excitement about his trip. It seemed absolutely insane, yet it was somehow one of the most reasonable things I'd done in ages. The maddening thing was that I was going to have to wait over a month for him to arrive.

I discussed the wisdom of his visit with my girlfriends. Their questions swam around in my brain each night as I struggled to sleep.

How much do you really know about him?

Is he going to stay in your apartment?

Are you sure he's not a serial killer?

The funny thing is, as we meet potential mates, we often know less about the men who end up in our beds than I knew about my California Dream. None of my friends could claim that they knew any of their lovers as well at their first meeting. Some of those lovers were now husbands.

My California Dream had always been kind and respectful. He was a friend. I was confident he'd cross no boundary that I put up.

Summer Again

It had been a year since my daily walks began and at least four months since I had actually taken one. I was feeling fat and the rising temperatures weren't helping with my hot flash-induced swelling. I began checking in with girlfriends about the progression of their hot flashes and the ability to sleep. Was it the change of seasons or a hormonal shift? I was getting no sleep at all.

My sleepless nights were spent worrying about the state of my body for my pending visitor as well as my imminent fiftieth birthday.

I made a few failed attempts to exercise and eat well. I only had three weeks before my California Dream arrived. I decided that my time would be best spent in general care and maintenance rather than attempting a complete overhaul.

I got my hands and feet buffed and polished and my body massaged. I had my hair cut. I was also sure to take care of the unwanted hair on my lip and chin as well as a good pruning of my unruly eyebrows.

The anticipation of his arrival was almost unbearable. In an effort to amuse myself and not put all of my hopes on a man who was truly geographically undesirable, I decided to go out on another museum date.

Jakarta Man

I once again searched the Internet for the elusive perfect man. I searched for the man who might be my missing link, the love of my life.

On my search through the Internet, I saw my potential love's profile and photo, and I decided the thing to do was to be bold and send the first communication. I sent him a cyber wink. There was a quick cryptic response, which I interpreted as a wry sense of humor. His correspondence alluded to world travels, living in Jakarta, and an interest in science. After the exchange of a few emails, we decided to meet at the American Museum of Natural History.

Date day arrived and I was excited at the prospect of meeting Jakarta Man. I decided a casual look of jeans was the way to go. Of course, careful consideration of layering also had to come into play in preparation for the hot flashes that were sure to come.

I arrived a few minutes early. It was a beautiful and sunny day, so I parked myself on the bench outside and perused the copy of the *New York Times* stashed in my bag. After a few minutes, a shadow appeared over the page. As I looked up, I saw a tall, handsome man who was casually well-dressed. He was backlit by the brilliant sun. Even so, at first glance, it was clear that this man was certainly more attractive than the photos he had posted on the Internet.

I was thrilled. Was it possible that a single, charming, witty, handsome man stood before me? I smiled at him as I stood and shook his hand in greeting. A soft hint of a long-forgotten Texas twang lingered in the air as he greeted me. What did I have to lose? Even if this man turned out to be a dud, I'd still have the dinosaurs to entertain me.

We wound our way through the museum. As we roamed from display to display, he began to tell me his life stories. He told me that his time spent in Jakarta involved a marriage, forced sex, corruption, millions of dollars, and rigged elections. These stories sounded more like a spy novel than real life. I wondered if they were real or the workings of a very smart madman?

The more he spoke, the more I caught glimpses of his rotting teeth. I had never seen anything like them before. It was remarkably distracting. I couldn't believe it! All I could think of was the song about Bloody Mary from *South Pacific*:

> *Bloody Mary's chewin' Betel nuts.*
> *She is always chewin' Betel nuts.*
> *Bloody Mary's chewin' Betel nuts.*
> *And she don't use Pepsodent!*

Had my Jakarta Man been chewing on Betel nuts? He told me he'd be going to the dentist the following Monday, and I wondered just how much could be done, short of a new pair of dentures.

I wanted to believe him, but, as the time passed,

his stories became more elaborate. Then he delivered the icing on the cake. He told me of the effort to slowly poison him to "keep him in his place." The poisoning had facilitated the rotting of his teeth while he was living in Jakarta.

I decided to dump Jakarta Man, stick with the dinosaurs and go back to a bit of California dreaming.

The Visit

My California Dream arrived late on a Thursday night. He called when he landed so I knew about what time he would arrive at my apartment. All of my girlfriends were on alert so they could check for signs of life in my apartment later in the evening and the next morning.

I turned out the lights in the kitchen and breakfast nook so I could see him as he stepped out of his cab. The moment I peeked out the window, there he was. He looked up and spotted me in the window. I smiled just as the doorman rang up to let me know that I had company.

He was a large man with long blond hair, a mustache and twinkling blue eyes. I was immediately comfortable having him in my home. Without thinking, we crawled into bed with each other and said goodnight. We were both tired, but we chatted through sleepy yawns and little kisses. We ended up making love and woke up the next morning in each other's arms.

For the next four days, we were inseparable. I showed him my New York, and he told me about his business and his family. When the time came, I was sad to see him go. We both wondered what in the hell we were doing with each other.

Clarinet Man

After my California Dream left, we talked on the phone several times a day. Despite our closeness, it seemed a bit ridiculous that I was even considering the idea of this very long-distance relationship. So, when my best friend called to let me know that her husband's friend had inquired about me and wanted my number, I agreed to meet him.

The Clarinet Man was age-appropriate, handsome and gainfully employed as a musician. We agreed to meet for a drink. A few days later, when he got out of a rehearsal, he drove to my place to pick me up. I invited him in for a glass of wine before we took a stroll to a neighborhood restaurant for a smart cocktail. He walked me home, kissed me goodnight, and went on his merry way.

He called me the following day and left messages about my beauty, charm, and wit. He asked when he could see me again. I was planning a trip to the West Coast to see my California Dream but I decided to see this handsome, geographically desirable man before I left.

We met for dinner, and we had a lovely time.

After dinner, I invited him up for a nightcap. I was caught off guard when he told me the saga of the failed relationship with his last girlfriend. He moved in to kiss me and then told me that he wasn't yet legally divorced and might still have feelings for his wife.

His wife.

"Did you think your feelings for your wife had an impact on the relationship with your ex-girlfriend?" I asked, not believing those words had just come from my lips.

He simply shrugged, and I sent him home.

Before I left for the West Coast, Clarinet Man called about going on another date with no indication as to whether he had changed his mind about the feelings he had for his wife. I was on my way to see my California Dream so I didn't respond.

Telling the Truth

I was excited about my trip to the West Coast to reconnect with my California Dream. He told me that, since our first meeting, he had lost weight, shaved his mustache, and cut his hair. We both wondered if I'd recognize him at the airport. I laughed out loud and suggested he wear a red carnation.

As I approached baggage claim in San Diego, I looked over the railing. I was immediately drawn to a man waiting below. I knew it was him. His spirit was beyond the physical. The moment I spied him, he looked up and saw me. We had an instant connection. We were at ease when we greeted each other. We held hands as we drove away from the airport. He drove to the marina where he kept his sailboat. It was a truly lovely sight. We were together a very short while before we collapsed into each other's arms and made love on the boat.

We left the boat and drove to his house to shower and change for dinner. The evening was lovely, but I couldn't keep quiet. He was the first man I had been with since The Bartender and I decided I had to tell him everything I had been up to over the last couple of years.

He was angry. He said he felt hurt and betrayed.

"Did you think you were dating a nun?"

He left the house in a huff and I was suddenly terrified that he wasn't coming back. I feared I'd be stranded in this strange house in Southern California. I didn't handle it in the best way, but it was in the only way I knew how. My California Dream came back two hours later. Neither of us slept. He lay down next to me in the bed fully clothed and stayed there the entire night.

He remained angry but civil for the remaining two days of my trip. His childishness annoyed me. In my presence, he talked to his friends on the phone about my visit and told them of my virtues and not my misadventures. Perhaps I had misread his feelings. I wanted to be with him. I wanted the opportunity to see if we truly were a fit for more than a week at a time. I heard him tell his friends that it was easy because I had a flexible business and a business partner. Despite that, we didn't discuss the expectations or the future. I was tired of dating, but I knew it would be foolhardy to put all of my eggs in this basket.

The next morning, we were both angry and hurt, so we spent our time exploring other issues like politics, race, immigration, and family. We picked fights about everything but the issue at hand. We made it through the day. Despite it all, we made every effort to be as normal as possible. That night, we went to the boat to sleep. As we curled up in bed, our small talk erupted into a huge fight. Neither of us was really listening to the other, and his anger erupted. After a lengthy discussion, we settled back into bed to try to get some sleep.

If I could have afforded it, I would have hopped on the next flight out. The next day was better. We were both more sensitive to each other's mood swings and did normal things. It was my last night in town, so he took me out to a lovely spot for dinner. It was a beautiful date. He was charming and loving, and he flirted madly. I flirted back, and I had a lovely time. After dinner, we collapsed into bed and went to sleep.

I wanted to kiss him all over and have him kiss me. In the middle of the night, he woke me up and made love to me. None of it made any sense. Clearly, we were not a good match, but we kept trying. Perhaps he was in menopause, too.

On the day I left, he was quiet. We drove to a national park. After taking in the beautiful view, he asked if I minded if we made a stop. I was surprised that he took me to help him find his father's grave and I am reminded that I have never visited my own father's grave.

My California Dream was nearly a nightmare, and I was barely feeling awake. As I prepared to fly home to my own reality, I was struck by the vastness of the land that separated us and by the spirit that drew us together. I was torn. What was our relationship? We did have a relationship of sorts, but it was hard to define when we were so far apart and I didn't like his moodiness or his anger.

I decided to pamper myself. With remaining frequent flyer mileage from my past life at the law firm, I upgraded to first class on the flight home. The combination of free wine, raging hormones, and hot flashes had me fighting back the tears. I wrote a tearful apology and poured out of my heart on my Blackberry. I knew he wouldn't receive it until I landed, but I found that it was something I had to write.

I wondered if I had I lost myself completely and what had compelled me to reach out to this man who had behaved so badly. As I was winging my way home, he left two loving voice mails for me that I received upon landing. We talked as soon as I was in the cab that would take me to my apartment.

Over the next few days, we talked regularly. Then he couldn't contain his ire. I was clearly the woman he cared for, and I was the woman he also now despised. He left for Mexico on business. I knew he was home now, and I hadn't heard from him. I had reached out to him, and he hadn't responded. I was dismayed by the fact that this was the same man whose heart seemed so big. I could understand that he no longer wanted to be my lover, but I couldn't reconcile the fact that he no longer wanted to be in my life at all after daily communication for six months.

I realized that the bigger concern should have been that I had any feelings for this man at all. I had looked so far from myself for my own happiness. The fact I told no one what actually happened on that trip was a red flag as to what a nightmare my California Dream really was.

Lost

I found myself in the odd position of being like the women I had criticized over the years, the women who gave themselves up in order to be with a man.

I wanted to have a man by my side to share the laughter and tears, but I wondered when I decided it was all right to make me be the price of admission. Perhaps it was my raging hormones, my reverse puberty, that pulled the trigger on my response to recent men. I remembered how girls in school would blush and change plans just because a boy called to say hello, even if he were a known scoundrel.

Those same boys grew up to be men. I learned a lot about their qualities over the last two years. They were womanizing, married, mean, inconsiderate, abusive, hateful, and rude.

I was having difficulty understanding why, after so many years of making every effort to weed those evildoers out of my life, I seemed to be including them at this late stage. I was taking myself so seriously on my path of rediscovery, that I seemed to have lost any sense of humor about dating.

Despite every effort to celebrate my birth festival,

my actual fiftieth birthday loomed large. I was suddenly terrified about being single. I had been happily single all my life, but the prospect of being single for the next phase of my life suddenly seemed untenable. I felt lost.

Does Mr. Right Exist?

What had me on this new path to disappointment? For the first time in my life, I was looking outside myself for my own happiness. I didn't think it was my pending fiftieth birthday, but I continued to self-medicate with carbohydrates. Rather than going out to greet whatever life had to offer, I found myself sipping scotch into the night while looking for the elusive Mr. Right on the Internet. As the days flew by and my jeans grew tighter, I wondered if I was really looking for Mr. Right or if I was looking for me.

I began my adventures in cyber dating a while back. I confess I haven't met anyone who is even close to being my Mr. Right. I dated men ranging in age from thirty-one to sixty-one, and men reaching far outside of that age spectrum have courted me. I discovered that men do all of the same things that women do. Men lie, cheat, love, cry, break my heart, and bring me joy.

Months ago, a potential handsome Mr. Right sent me an email. He saw my online photo and liked what he saw in my profile. After the exchange of several emails, he took a closer look and honestly said he wanted someone younger. It wasn't meant to be hurtful. He merely stated his case. He wanted a life with a white picket fence. That included marriage, dog, and children. I was never going to be his Ms. Right. My biological clock had been broken years ago. Even if it were in working order, time had run out anyway. There would be no children squeaked out of me.

I was so full of hope that there was a Mr. Right for everyone. After discussions with a friend that I thought might be more appropriate, I decided to contact Mr. Right and suggest he meet her instead. Much to my surprise, I received an email from him asking about her. I wrote back words of encouragement. What did he have to lose? The worse thing that could happen would be that he was entertained over a cup of coffee.

Wanna Play Doctor?

Suddenly, after what seemed like months of inactivity, my Internet dating mailbox was filling up. Men of all shapes, ages, and sizes seemed to be lining up with winks, smiles, and emails.

Each time a new piece of mail arrived, I found some reason to reject it. He was too young or old, short or tall, thin or fat, conservative or liberal, or mean or nice. In any event, it was an oddity for a truly educated professional man to be found in the cyber world. I received an email from a gentleman who said he was a mere four years older than me. He was a doctor, a surgeon at a major hospital in New York. He said he'd like to correspond with me. How could I possibly resist? Because of his position, he hadn't posted a picture, but he readily sent one upon my request.

He was very matter-of-fact and to the point. He was a busy man who was looking for a woman. The Doctor got straight to the point. He wanted a long-term relationship with a woman who was smart, attractive, and loved sex.

I thought, "*Me. Me. Me!*"

After a couple of conversations, I agreed to meet him for dinner. You'd think I had learned my lesson after my disastrous dinner date with the Athlete who gave me candy kisses and the gift of Lady Stetson, but I agreed to dine with the Doctor. My big mistake was in not Googling him before our date. If I had, I would have discovered that he was far beyond the fifty-four years he claimed to be.

The Doctor selected a lovely bistro on the East Side of Manhattan near the hospital. He had warned me that he was performing a complex surgery that day and might need to cancel. He called to confirm that afternoon. I could feel him beaming through the phone. His surgery had gone well, and he was in the mood to celebrate and boast.

I arrived at the restaurant a few minutes early and ordered a glass of wine at the bar. It was a lovely spot, a little restaurant that was clearly family-run and designed for a tryst. Just as I took the first sip from my glass of wine, I felt a man standing next to me. I looked up to see a much shorter, older version of the man I had been corresponding with.

"What the hell," I murmured.

I was about to have dinner with a very smart and charming man who was bursting from the fantastic day he'd had. The hostess showed us to our table, and we ordered a lovely meal. He was smart and charming, and we had quite a bit in common. He actually listened to what I had to say and showed an interest in my favorite New York pastimes, the American Museum of Natural History and the theater. He was perfectly charming and seemingly harmless. I began to wonder who I knew that would be more appropriate for this man. He had lied about his age, but surely someone I knew should date this successful doctor.

As he paid the bill, he asked if I'd like a ride home. Typically, I wouldn't allow a first date to know where I lived, but this seemed perfectly reasonable and chaste. As we left the restaurant, I was reminded that, despite global warming, it was quite cold outside. I took his arm for warmth as he walked me to his car. We chatted easily on the way home. I was surprised when he removed my glove to kiss my hand. His fingers played with the skin on the back of my hand. I didn't take my hand away. I'm not sure why. I think I was surprised at the change in demeanor.

We arrived at my building, and he stopped the car to say goodnight. It suddenly became clear that he thought he was coming upstairs. He thought dinner had entitled him to a Viagra pass. I leaned over to say goodnight and give him a little kiss. Then he grabbed me. It was pleasant actually. He was a very good kisser, and I responded to him. Then, realizing my predicament, I thought it was time to get out of the car. He grabbed me and kissed me hard, shoving my hand in his lap. I knew my doorman was watching every second, so I felt safe. My mind immediately went to the episode of *Sex and the City* where Samantha dated the older man for presents. I closed my eyes tightly to see if all men were the same in the dark. In many ways, they are. Then I remembered the scene where Samantha ran from her lover's apartment after seeing his wrinkly butt. Could I have sex for presents? Could I learn to enjoy this smart and charming, yet shrunken and bald, man? The answer was no.

The Doctor was confident. He truly believed that

he'd undoubtedly spend the night in my bed. It was time to make my escape. Before he let me go, he grabbed me and kissed me hard and passionately. Moving my head, he darted his tongue in my ear. The Doctor grabbed my hand and pressed it into his lap and rubbed it against his growing erection. He wanted me now and told me so. I suggested that, if he wanted me so badly, he'd have to wait. He'd have to plan ahead.

For days, he called me, wondering how I was and when he'd see me again. I finally had to tell him to stop. He said he kept calling because he was worried about us. I didn't realize that there was an us.

I took a deep breath and simply said, "I'll just have to say no. This isn't going to happen. Don't call me again."

I didn't want to play doctor with the Doctor.

Don't Bring Your Toys to the Table

The Doctor made it clear that it was time to stop taking myself so seriously. It was summer in New York, and there was really nothing quite like it. Central Park and the weather were absolutely divine.

The summer heat had me feeling like I had a fever. I roamed the streets, searching for the next air-conditioned doorway, always with a bottle of cold water in my hand. It was also possible that my hormones were running amok since my hot flashes were picking up again and my ability to multitask was diminishing.

It could have been menopause, but it wasn't just me. Clearly everyone had the fever because my email box was bursting at the seams. Most of the mail was ridiculous banter from men who couldn't even complete a full sentence. I quickly went through them, hitting the delete key. Then there was an email that was different. He seemed to be clever, smart, and charming! Could this be possible?

We decided to join each other in an instant messaging session. Within minutes, he had me in fits of laughter. He said he was just a couple years older than I was. He said he had no idea how to post an electronic picture to the Web. We chatted easily for some time with occasional bursts of laughter. Impulsively, he asked if I'd meet him. He'd come to wherever I wanted, and he'd buy me dinner. I stopped dead in my tracks. I was sure the word "no" was forming on my lips, but I surprised myself by saying yes.

The weather was lovely, so I put on a low-cut, frilly blouse, a skirt, and heels. My makeup looked great, and I was having a good hair day. Even my doorman, who rarely spoke, commented on my appearance as I left the building.

Ever hopeful, I walked into the restaurant smiling. What I saw was a horrible, old, fat, bald, and ugly man looking at me with a big grin on his face. I don't use any of those words lightly, but I couldn't believe my eyes. If he was truly only fifty-four, the years had been very unkind to him. I had apparently agreed to have dinner with Santa's evil twin.

It was one of my favorite restaurants. He had been funny and charming in his writing, so I decided to buck up and make the best of it. I ordered a drink, and we perused the menu. As we were waiting for our orders to arrive, he looked at me and regaled me with one of the most vulgar stories I had heard in some time. It was certainly the most vulgar story I had ever heard uttered by a stranger. I was stunned that within minutes of meeting this bad Santa was telling me a story about golden showers and fisting at the dinner table. I briefly considered standing up and walking out, but I was too curious.

"Does that story work for you?" I asked. "Do you

actually find women are charmed by that story?"

He admitted he didn't know why he had told me the story, but he alluded to how he felt it defined submission. Then he quickly apologized as dinner arrived. We discovered that we actually did have a lot in common, and we had a lively conversation about the theater.

Dinner was finally over. I thought I made it very clear that I wasn't interested in any further communication with this evil Santa. He paid the bill. As we left the restaurant, he made it obvious that he intended to come to my apartment. As he said so, I noticed that he picked up the bag of toys he had brought with him. This bad Santa actually believed I was going to allow him to take me home, restrain me, and do God knows what.

A cab finally arrived, and I jumped in. I couldn't believe he jumped in beside me. I made it clear that he wasn't coming over, but he still thought it was appropriate that his sausage-fingered hand should fall on my thigh. I had given this date considerable thought. Was I really that gullible? Did I look as stupid as that? Did he really think I'd let him come over and tie me up? I guess I'll never know. No matter what the answer is, there is one thing that is clear. Any man who may be reading this should know that there is no situation where it is appropriate to bring your toys to the dinner table.

Taking Pause

It was time for a little reflection. I counted my blessings and realized I was just a few short weeks away from my birthday. I was more than relieved that I could wear skirts and T-shirts rather than try to pour myself into my too tight jeans. I tried to cut back on bread and increase my water intake. My goal of having legs like Tina Turner for my birthday had been lost. Even so, I now started exercising and explored what had caused me to derail. What had caused me to let go of all that was good in me?

I called my girlfriends, the ones who truly loved me, and asked what they saw. I wondered if they doubted themselves these days. Was it hormones and hot flashes or a natural part of approaching this landmark that made us all doubt ourselves?

We wondered if we mattered.

We worried about each other and cried.

We worried about our parents and cried.

We worried about the state of the world and cried.

I wasn't alone. We were all worried. We just had to learn to accept the fact that joy could be found despite our doubts and fears or, perhaps, because of them.

I spent the last year leading up to my birthday celebrating this birth festival year and realized how much love I gave and received from my friends. I wondered why I thought I needed more. While these friends who loved me bolstered me up, I had insisted on seeking the key to my happiness in men who were wrong for me, men who were unavailable, didn't really care about the love of a good woman, or didn't really like a woman of ideals. I spent my life avoiding these men.

Enough was enough. It was time to get back to searching for my own bliss.

I Wiped My Mouth

Once again, I've got my eye on the prize. I am focused. My mother would say that I'm 'on the prowl.' I say that I am looking for the last great love of my life. I have begun to date again.

About a month ago the Wino, a wine importer, asked me to join him for a drink. I agreed to meet him and gave this date a quick twenty minutes – just long enough to sip a glass of wine and decide whether or not I wanted to meet again for a full-length date. The bar he selected was dark but homey. We had just enough time for him to tell me how wonderful he was and to regale me with his vast knowledge of wine. I was a bit concerned that I didn't get a chance to really get a good look at him in the low light and then realized that the light was probably more than flattering for me.

There certainly wasn't a spark, but as I ran out the door I agreed to meet him again for another date. The Wino diligently called and e-mailed for 3 weeks until I agreed to meet him at a museum. I had been on my feet all day, and arriving less than five minutes before the appointed time, plunked myself down on the bench in the entry letting out a deep sigh.

The Wino walked in and spotted me immediately. In this light he was clearly of a much older vintage than he had claimed. He swaggered over and frowned.

"You were early," he chided.

"I like to be on time."

His face was a bit crooked and gnarly so I couldn't be sure if he scowled, smirked or smiled before he darted into the crowd toward the entrance, expecting me to follow. He directed me through the museum pointing and lecturing as though I had never seen art before.

"You see, this is a painting."

"Ah," I cried.

"And this. This is called sculpture."

"Ah," I cried.

"Here we have a drawing."

"Ah," I cried.

"Would you like a glass of wine?"

"Yes," I cried.

As he led me out of the museum I thought briefly about cutting and running, but decided that at the very least the Wino could select a lovely glass of wine before I went home.

While he claimed to be just a couple of years older, I was sure that he was much older than I. The Wino ordered a couple of appetizers as he ordered our wine selection. Clearly he thought the date was going well.

By the time the date was over, I was bored out of my brain. He rambled on about God knows what and never once even pretended to listen to a word I had to say.

When we parted he kissed me and as the door to my cab closed, I involuntarily wiped my mouth. I don't think I've done that since the Seventh Grade.

No more dates with the Wino for me.

I wiped my mouth!

The Irishman

My first date with The Irishman was a quick after work drink with a time limit. I've had a lot of practice dating and realized that there is absolutely no such thing as cyber chemistry. We had exchanged a couple of emails and chatted on the phone but it was time to see if there was really anything there.

We agreed to meet for a drink and both had someplace else to go when our hour was up. I, of course, arrived first and ordered my favorite smart cocktail, a scotch and water. He arrived with a big smile on his face, sat down next to me and then ordered a beer. I was surprised how easily we chatted. We covered everything from politics and religion to children and love. As he teased me about my liberal leanings, a big grin appeared, letting me know he was pulling my leg, and he leaned over to kiss me. Just a lovely little kiss that made me keenly aware that I'd like to have a few more of them. Suddenly it was time to go. The Irishman paid for our drinks and then we walked for a couple of blocks before we parted with another quick kiss.

A couple of days later he called to say that he had

the day off and wondered if I could meet for breakfast. Work was too busy, but I let him know I would be free for a late lunch and a walk in the park.

As I watched The Irishman walk toward me on the street, he seemed more attractive than I had remembered. Perhaps it was his height and strong gait, or perhaps those quick, sweet kisses had been working their magic behind my brain. Whatever the reason was, as we walked up the street gabbing away, I realized how lovely it was to be in the company of The Irishman.

We stopped at a local restaurant for a snack, then made our way to the park. As we walked, chattering away about this and that, I directed him to a spot where the view was particularly lovely and he leaned down to kiss me. It was soft and lovely and I kissed him back. I love holding hands and little public displays of affection. We walked a bit further and he kissed me again as we wound our way out of the park and back on to the street. I took his hand for a while, enjoying the feeling of his large rough hand in mine.

As he walked me home, I knew we had a few more minutes before he had to go, so I suggested getting some water and sitting in the back garden until it was time for him to go. The Irishman accompanied me upstairs and then as I was taking bottled water from the fridge, he kissed me. This time it was a long and wet kiss and I fell into it. I tried to restrain myself and stiffened my body beneath his touch. It was ridiculous really. I found him remarkably sexy. He was funny and handsome and easy to talk to. I wanted nothing more than for him to have his way with me, but I didn't want to screw it up by screwing him too soon.

"*Leave him wanting more,*" was the only thought in my mind.

The moment that thought passed through my brain, he kissed my neck and his hands passed over my breasts. I responded by feeling his powerful arms as I kissed him.

The Irishman's hands moved down my body and reached between my legs, teasing me over the fabric of my leggings.

"Stop," I said pulling his hand away and then leaning in to kiss him again.

His hand reached back down between my legs as his mouth devoured mine.

"Stop."

"All right, then."

We sat down at my table so he could show me his home in Ireland on the computer and then he turned my chair around to face him and kissed me again. As I leaned over to return his kiss, his hands cupped my breasts. I protested and said we should go outside. He helped me to my feet and then took my hands and held them out from my body, pressing me up against the wall, leaning into me and kissing my neck, his hard body against mine.

"Let me see you. Let me see your breasts."

Then he pulled his shirt over his head and kissed me. I loved the feel of his powerful chest and reached up and touch his nipples. He responded with a lovely intake of breath and I knew he liked it. I continued to play with his nipples as we kissed, first both, then one.

"You drive me wild when you touch them both at the same time." I happily obliged. As he kissed me he backed me through my apartment and tried to take me to my bedroom.

"No."

"Why not?"

"I'm not ready to be naked."

"But I don't know how long it will be before I can see you again."

"All the more reason to keep my clothes on," I thought.

I took his hand and led him to the living room sofa and straddled his lap and leaned down to kiss him again. I kept saying no, but couldn't get enough of him. I could feel him growing harder beneath me and me growing wet between my legs. His hand reached around behind me, and slipped inside my leggings. I felt my body quiver as his fingers began to work their magic. I couldn't remember the last time a man made me feel so sexy. I kept saying no but truly wanted him. I let him touch me until I was on the verge of orgasm and then pulled away. If I was going to deny The Irishman, I was going to deny myself as well. We kissed and played, The Irishman bare-chested and me fully clothed until he had to go.

I spent the rest of the day thinking about his kisses and smelling his delicious scent on body. He called to say he had a lovely time and to wish me a productive weekend. The whole time he spoke, all I could think of was how nice it would be to have him spoon me as I fell asleep.

I hope to see The Irishman again soon. I doubt that my willpower will be as strong the next time. In fact, perhaps I'll just invite him over for a meal at home and serve myself for dessert.

Falling

The Irishman called the following day and asked to see me again. I suggested he come over for dinner and that I'd cook for him. When he arrived, the house was filled with the aroma of roasting chicken and potatoes and a hint of the apple crisp cooling on the rack. He smiled broadly at me as he came in the door. I kissed him lightly and offered him a glass of wine.

"I think the bird is nearly ready to come out of the oven," I said as I opened the oven door. As I bent over to check the progress of my chicken, I was sure I heard him growl. I took the bird out and closed the oven door.

Before I could turn around his rough hands grabbed my hips and pulled me towards him. He thrust his hips into mine and kissed my neck. His hands moved from my hips to my breasts and he easily found my hardening nipples and gave them a pinch. I turned around to kiss him and he pulled his shirt over his head and smiled. Clearly we were going to start the evening with dessert.

I took his hand and led him to my bedroom. I took off my clothes for him and watched him watch me. I stepped over and unzipped his jeans, then pulled them down over his hard ass then grabbed a hold of his huge cock. He picked me up and threw me back on the bed and climbed on top of me. He held my hands over my head and kissed me. I could feel him hard against my leg.

"Condoms?" he asked.

"There," I said pointing to the nightstand. In a second it was on and in two seconds he was inside of me. His body was muscled and strong as he pushed into me. I was eager for him and raised my hips to meet his with each thrust. Remembering our last date, I reached up to his chest and stroked his nipples. He cried out and quickly came. He collapsed beside me and seemed a little embarrassed, covering us both with the duvet. I smiled and nuzzled against him and let him nap for 15 minutes as he spooned me. I rolled over and kissed him awake.

"Hungry?" I asked.

"Starving."

I kissed his lovely mouth and then leaned down to kiss his chest. At the touch of his nipples, his penis sprang back to life.

"They're like on switches," I giggled.

All he could do was answer with a sharp intake of breath.

I kissed my way down his belly and took him into my mouth for just a moment. As he groaned, I climbed between his legs and squeezed my breasts around his erection and rocked until he came again.

He went into the bathroom for a shower before dinner. I was going to join him, but to my surprise he had locked the door. I showered in the other bathroom and then put on a sarong and went to set the table for dinner. When he came into the kitchen he gave my behind a little swat and grinned broadly.

"You're a beautiful woman."

"You're not so bad yourself."

"I love that thing you're wearing."

"A sarong."

"Nice," he said touching the knot between my breasts. I reached out to touch is bare chest and he backed away.

"Oh no you don't. I want some of that chicken first."

I laughed and cooed as he ate his fill of chicken and potatoes. We made love twice more before he left and made plans to see each other again, this time with his daughter for the weekend.

Two days later he arrived with a bag and a beautiful eight-year-old girl who had his blue eyes. We played house the whole weekend. Each night after he put her to sleep for the evening in the guest room,he'd sneak into my room and wake me with a kiss. After a few kisses and nibbling on my nipples, his hand would always reach down and find me wet and ready for him. I loved his size and forcefulness in bed. He'd throw me around, shifting my body into new positions until we both collapsed from the sheer exercise of it all, then he would slip back to his daughter's room.

After a few weeks he stopped returning to her room. In the middle of the night I would hear the pitter patter of little feet come into my room, climb up between us and curl up against me until morning.

I was falling in love with playing house.

Cutting My Losses

Things with The Irishman seemed to be going pretty well. He's fun, kind, helpful, hardworking, sexy, and he's a single dad with more baggage than I could dream of having. In spite of his very heavy steamer trunk, I decided to climb aboard his ship and test the waters.

Before I knew what was happening, I fell madly in love with his little girl. The first time her big blue eyes looked up at me as she hugged me and said, "I love you," I was a goner. Of course, she is too young to understand that Daddy is dating. Frankly, I don't think she should know. She still dreams of her parents' reconciliation and *The Parent Trap* is her favorite movie. Of course that doesn't stop me from fantasizing about him grabbing me in his strong arms, telling me he can't live without me and whisking me away to his precious Emerald Isle.

I have asked myself over and over again whether or not I would have continued to see The Irishman if I hadn't fallen head over heels with his daughter. There is no way to know. They are a package deal and he has the same eyes.

I am caught between a rock and a hard place.

The passage of time has made my doubts grow deep and my fantasies grow strong. My own life is upside down these days and I am looking for the key, buried ages ago, to my own steamer trunk. The Irishman and I have only been seeing each other for a short while, yet the involvement of family and child and the shared details that have been locked up tight in his steamer trunk of baggage seem to have accelerated the opening of my heart, my need to know where I stand, the need to declare "us."

I want to pack my own bags of baggage and brace for the ride, but he has not offered a ticket and I think that, for this leg of his journey, he must sail alone. Should I be patient, enjoy the ride and wait for him to be ready. I'm left wondering if it is time to cut my losses and run.

Cutting His Losses

I was excited to see The Irishman and his daughter each weekend. To my surprise, he came over alone one Friday evening and called it quits. Despite my own fears and doubts, I confess I didn't see it coming.

"I just can't," he said.

As it turns out, The Irishman's steamer trunk is filled with rocks and is sinking fast. He is too overwhelmed to be in a relationship at the moment, so he wants to be my friend.

What is our 'relationship'? I was waiting to talk about it, to give it a name we both felt comfortable with; he had already named it, become overwhelmed and needed to rename it.

I didn't know it, but I had been dubbed 'girlfriend'. His friends knew. He told his sister. He had even told his mother! No wonder his mother was eager to meet me during her short visit from Ireland the week before.

The Irishman brought his sister and mother over for tea. I made sure the house was sparkling and baked a picture-perfect apple pie. I loved meeting them and had a fabulous time. Before they left, cameras came out and many photos were snapped with the promise of sharing them in the future. There were questions about whether or not I would be visiting Ireland.

There was no way for me to know, but apparently The Irishman had already decided.

"I just can't," he said.

I asked why he had gone to the trouble of introducing me to his family if he felt we should 'end' things, and he said that his mother wanted to meet me, his girlfriend, and that he wanted her to meet me. The introduction to his family only made my fantasies run wilder than they had the week before. He should have never allowed that meeting to happen and I was angry about it.

I cried the morning I put away his daughter's toothbrush for safekeeping. I supposed I should have thrown it away, but that seemed to final an act. I'm in love with that little girl and her big blue eyes that look so much like her Daddy's.

My fantasies of being whisked away by a pair of strong arms have been dashed. I am sad and so is The Irishman. We both cried as he left.

He hopes that we can still be friends.

He hopes we can still be in each other's lives.

Then the truth came out. I turns out there was another woman who had suddenly returned after having been out of town for several months.

The Irishman wants to know if we can meet for drinks after work. He has got to be kidding.

Back to the Beginning

I am middle-aged.
I am an older woman.
People call me "ma'am."
I came of age for the first time in New York City when I moved from North Dakota nearly thirty years ago. Now that I am fifty, I find I have come of age again. Things never work out as you have planned them, but I have found myself, and I am happy. While it is true that I thought I grew up years ago, I find that the truth is that, if you do it right, you never stop growing. I have rediscovered my sexuality and learned to love my body. I also uncovered some of the secrets that made me protect my own heart so fiercely. Amazingly, as a result, I became more willing to expose my soft underbelly and open my heart to whatever arrows come my way.

I see beauty in the rain outside my window and now cry from the sheer joy and beauty of nature rather than the rush of hormones surging through my body. I still cry regularly, and I am still learning that it is safe to allow myself to be vulnerable.

What no one ever tells you is that there is no

secret. We must each find our paths to happiness and never look to someone else to make us whole. That said, always allow for the fact that unconditional love can make us better than we ever dreamed we could be. I am trying very hard to allow that love into my life. While we are here, the most important thing to learn is that we all deserve to let someone love us.

I remain hopefully ever after.

About the Author

Michelle Churchill is a single woman living in New York where she hosts extravagant dinner parties and always makes a smart cocktail.